Essentials of Corporate Governance

Theoretical Foundations and Practical Application

By Dr. Charchafa Ilyes

2025

Published by Charchafa Ilyes
Finance and Accounting Department, University of Setif 1

Available through multiple distribution channels.

First printing, 2025.

DEDICATION

To my parents, whose unwavering support and love have been the foundation of my journey.

To my sisters and brother, for their endless encouragement and companionship.

And to all my students, whose curiosity and enthusiasm inspire me every day.

PREFACE

The journey to writing "Essentials of Corporate Governance" has been a deeply rewarding and enlightening experience, grounded in both my academic research and practical teaching. My thesis, completed several years ago, laid the foundation for this work, providing a comprehensive exploration of corporate governance. Since then, I have had the privilege of teaching this subject to numerous students, each cohort contributing to my understanding and appreciation of the complexities and nuances of corporate governance.

The inspiration for this book stems from the dynamic and evolving nature of corporate governance, as well as the insightful discussions and questions raised by my students over the years. Their enthusiasm and curiosity have continually motivated me to delve deeper into the subject and refine my teaching methods.

This book aims to provide a thorough yet accessible guide to the essential principles and practices of corporate governance. It is designed not only for students but also for practitioners and anyone interested in understanding the mechanisms that drive good governance in corporations. The material presented here reflects a synthesis of academic research, practical examples, and my own experiences in the field.

I am deeply grateful to my parents, whose unwavering support has been a constant source of strength. My sisters and brother have provided endless encouragement and companionship, for which I am profoundly thankful. I also wish to extend my heartfelt thanks to my colleagues and mentors, whose insights and feedback have been invaluable in shaping this work.

To my students, past and present, this book is dedicated to you. Your passion for learning and your probing questions have significantly contributed to the content and quality of this book. I hope this work will serve as a valuable resource in your academic and professional endeavors.

As you explore the pages of "Essentials of Corporate Governance," I trust you will find it both informative and engaging. May it inspire you to think critically and contribute to the ongoing discourse on corporate governance.

With gratitude and appreciation,
Charchafa Ilyes

TABLE OF CONTENTS

Introduction

INTRODUCTION

The financial crises in Southeast Asian nations in 1997 and the failure of major American and European companies led to difficulties in attracting enough investment and capital for operations. These crises and failures were attributed to poor management, financial misconduct, inefficient use of available resources, lack of transparency and adequate fair disclosure in accounting reports due to failed control systems, and the large gap between executive pay and financial performance coupled with unethical practices at the companies.

As a result, investors became reluctant to invest their money after suffering heavy financial losses, prompting them to clearly state their unwillingness to bear the consequences of corruption and mismanagement. Before investing, investors began requesting evidence that companies seeking their capital adopt sound, rational management and administration practices.

This prompted many countries and international organizations to search for mechanisms enabling access to these good practices to protect investors and other stakeholders from the malpractices by boards of directors. These mechanisms became known as corporate governance practices or mechanisms through which companies should be managed and operated.

The concept of corporate governance refers to a set of general frameworks that regulate relationships between various parties related to the company, including management, shareholders, and other stakeholders (customers, suppliers, employees, accounting and auditing firms, etc.). This ultimately ensures integrity of the company's management, achievement of objectives, adherence to ethical standards, and compliance with laws and regulations.

These challenges have prompted organizations to pay unprecedented attention to corporate governance, whether by professionals or researchers. Corporate governance has become an essential training field for university students, emerging as a vital and necessary course. Therefore, this book aims to present scientific material covering the disciplines in which the subject of corporate governance falls. The following outlines the learning objectives and required knowledge acquisitions.

Learning objectives: After reading this book, the reader will be able to:

- Identify different corporate governance concepts and approaches.
- Identify and distinguish theories explaining corporate governance and orientations.
- Recognize differences in governance practices between common global systems and models.
- Understand the procedures and steps for proper corporate governance practice.
- Measure, evaluate and assess governance practice in economic and financial companies.

Required Knowledge: Understanding this book's themes requires prior student knowledge in:

- Business Management
- Financial Accounting
- Financial Management
- Financial Markets

CHAPTER 1
CORPORATE GOVERNANCE CONCEPTUAL FRAMEWORK

Chapter 1: Corporate Governance Conceptual Framework

In this chapter, we will elucidate the concept of governance by examining researchers' diverse perspectives on a unified definition. Additionally, we will outline the value framework upon which this concept is grounded.

1. Definition of Corporate Governance

Governance encompasses oversight and control, particularly in the prevention and management of corruption. Given its association with multiple fields such as accounting, finance, economics, management, social sciences, and politics, as well as its relevance to various internal and external stakeholders, definitions of governance vary based on the author's perspective regarding its relationship to those fields and parties.

Shleifer and Vishny (1997) perceive corporate governance as addressing how financiers ensure they receive returns on their investments and how they monitor and prevent management from misappropriating funds or investing in unprofitable ventures to safeguard against financial losses.

Keong Low (2002) regards corporate governance "as an environment where individuals in control of a company provide quality management to advance the performance of the company in the interests of all shareholders, regardless of whether they are minority or majority shareholders."

Mathiesen (2002) defines corporate governance as a "field in economics that investigates how to secure/motivate efficient management of corporations by the use of incentive mechanisms, such as contracts, organizational designs and legislation. This is often limited to the question of improving financial performance, for example, how the corporate owners can secure/motivate that the corporate managers will deliver a competitive rate of return".

John and Senbet (1998) regard corporate governance as dealing with mechanisms by which stakeholders of a corporation exercise control over corporate insiders and management to ensure their interests are protected. This perspective aligns with the definition provided by the Institute of Internal Auditors (IIA) (2002), which characterizes governance processes as dealing with the procedures utilized by representatives of the organization's stakeholders to oversee risk and control processes administered by management. Monitoring organizational risks and ensuring that controls adequately mitigate those risks contribute directly to achieving organizational goals and preserving organizational value. Those performing governance activities are accountable to the organization's stakeholders for effective stewardship.

In the same vein, Demirag et al. (2000) define corporate governance as a "framework for effective monitoring, regulation, and control of companies, which allows alternative internal and external mechanisms for achieving the underlying objectives."

The definitions provided by Shleifer and Vishny (1997), Keong Low (2002), and Mathiesen (2002) align with the so-called narrow view of corporate governance. This perspective suggests that the company's responsibility is confined to safeguarding shareholder interests and maximizing financial returns. Such a viewpoint is rooted in the agency theory framework.

Conversely, the definitions provided by John and Senbet (1998), the American Institute of Internal Auditors (2002), and Demirag et al. (2000) align with the wider view of corporate governance. This perspective suggests that the company's responsibility extends beyond solely safeguarding shareholder interests to also encompass the interests of other stakeholders, as well as considerations of social and environmental factors alongside economic ones. It is grounded in the stakeholder theory framework.

In parallel, Rezaee (2009) highlighted that the primary objective of socially responsible companies is to generate long-term value, facilitated by corporate governance frameworks. According to the researcher, this involves two aspects: value creation and value protection. In terms of value creation, the focus is on shareholders through the implementation of long-term strategies aimed at sustaining performance. As for value protection, the emphasis lies on ensuring accountability in management and control to safeguard the interests of both shareholders and stakeholders.

Consequently, the concept of corporate governance according to the narrow perspective may make the outcome of governance practice dependent solely on value creation for the company. In contrast, the wide view of corporate governance adds value protection in addition to value creation. This recognizes that a company exists to sustain itself, and its continuity depends not just on creating value but also preserving it. This continuity serves as a common ground for the interests of all the company's stakeholders. It can be argued that the wide view is more comprehensive than the narrow view, as it emphasizes value preservation, which implies the company's survival and continuity. The outcome of governance practices under this wide view ensures the company's long-term value, rather than confining itself to value creation alone, which, if limited to that aspect, could jeopardize the company's survival and continuity.

From a positive perspective, the wide view of corporate governance is bolstered by the evolving perspectives of prominent developers of governance practices. In his renowned 1992 report "The financial aspects of corporate governance", Cadbury defined governance as "the system by which companies are directed and controlled. Boards of directors are responsible for the governance of their companies……The responsibilities of the board include setting the company's strategic aims, providing the leadership to put them into effect, supervising the management of the business and reporting to shareholders on their stewardship. The board's actions are subject to laws, regulations and the shareholders in general meeting".

However, in 1999 Governance Overview report of the World Bank, Cadbury provided another definition: "Corporate governance is concerned with holding the balance between economic and social goals and between individual and communal goals...the aim is to align as nearly as possible the interests of individuals, corporations and society". In this second definition, Cadbury demonstrated that the goal of governance is to balance stakeholder and societal interests in general, while simultaneously stressing the importance of adopting the corporate social responsibility concept alongside economic considerations. This marked a fundamental shift in Cadbury's perspective, which initially confined governance's goal to protecting shareholder interests. This revised definition emerged after numerous crises occurred in the 1990s, perhaps most notably the financial crisis that affected Southeast Asian countries. Sullivan (2009) also believes that Cadbury's expanded view of governance emerged from the standpoint that corruption results from poor governance. Accordingly, it can be argued that the narrow corporate governance view may not reflect good governance practice, while the opposite holds true if it aligns with the wide view.

When describing governance as a system, it's essential to analyze the components that constitute this system. Based on the literature on corporate governance, the concept can be elucidated through the following:

- **System Inputs:**
  - Legal, economic, financial, social, and ethical requirements stemming from the provision of resources to the company.
  - Delegation of authority to management as per contractual terms.
- **Processing:**
  - Addressing these requirements or managing these elements
  - Oversight by internal parties such as the board of directors, board committees, and internal auditors
  - Involvement of external parties such as financial markets, government/professional bodies, and external auditors

- Grounded in ethical conduct, control mechanisms, and risk management practices

- **System Outputs:**
  - Safeguarding the interests of the company's stakeholders, including shareholders, lenders, customers, employees, and society at large
  - Achieved within a framework of accountability, fairness, disclosure, and transparency

2. Objectives and Importance of Corporate Governance

According to a study by the Center for International Private Enterprise (CIPE) (2002) on establishing corporate governance practices, good corporate governance aids companies and the overall economy in attracting investments and bolstering long-term economic performance and competitiveness through several methods:

- By emphasizing transparency in accounting, auditing, procurement processes/procedures, and all institutional transactions/operations, it fights corruption (which wastes resources, reduces competitiveness, and drives away investors).
- Corporate governance practices play a vital role in improving management effectiveness by assisting managers and boards in developing sound strategies, making careful decisions regard ng mergers and acquisitions, and aligning rewards with performance. These practices contribute to attracting investment on favorable terms and enhancing company efficiency.
- By adopting transparency standards in dealings with investors and debtors, a robust corporate governance system can play a crucial role in preventing banking crises, even in countries where most companies don't actively operate in financial markets.
- Recent research suggests that countries implementing protections for minority shareholders tend to have more liquid capital markets. In contrast, countries

with weak shareholder protection systems often witness a concentration of ownership under a small group of investors.

- Applying corporate governance strengthens public confidence in privatization processes, helping ensure the state achieves optimal returns on investments leading to more job opportunities and economic development.

The importance of good corporate governance for each stakeholder can be highlighted as follows:

- **For Investors:** It safeguards their rights, ensuring that investments are productive, sustainable, and profitable. It fosters accountability, transparency, fairness, and efficiency standards, thereby bolstering confidence and security. Governance establishes checks and balances that consider stakeholder interests, including those of shareholders. Enhanced governance correlates with improved performance, reducing the likelihood of misconduct against shareholders. Additionally, it grants shareholders a voice in board matters, safeguarding their long-term interests.
- **For Management:** Effective governance necessitates contemporary oversight methods aimed at regulating the conduct of those in leadership positions. This empowers management to fulfill their responsibilities towards the company and society in accordance with legal requirements and ethical values. It amplifies productivity, profitability, viability, competitiveness, credibility, and reputation. Governance furnishes guidelines that ensure the organization operates efficiently, effectively, and sustainably.
- **For Employees:** Good governance establishes permanent, secure job opportunities that provide purchasing power to support families, cover expenses, finance pensions and healthcare, and enable investment. This stimulates the development of goods and services markets and facilitates wealth creation. Effective governance ensures organizational growth, thereby fostering future job and position opportunities.

- **For Consumers:** Good governance guarantees the availability of high-quality products at the lowest prices, as well as the provision of goods and services as needed.
- **For Government:** Good governance promotes enhanced productivity and the efficient and effective utilization of resources within a responsible framework. It entails transparent disclosure and reporting through accounting practices, facilitating faster tax collection. Additionally, it encourages foreign investment, facilitates wealth creation, and ensures equitable distribution of resources.
- **For Society:** Good governance leads to improved living standards, ensuring the fulfillment of basic needs and requirements for a decent life. It also ensures that organisations add value by responding to community interests and upholding the principles of fairness, transparency, and accountability. Furthermore, it promotes the efficient and effective use of resources provided by the community.

Based on the above, it can be stated that the importance of governance lies in driving the company towards responsibility in its various forms:

- **Economic Responsibility:**
  - Ensures the company prioritizes performance to maximize its value and generate necessary profits.
  - Focuses on creating and sustaining a competitive advantage over other companies.
  - Achieves high levels of efficiency in management, operations, and productivity.
- **Social Responsibility:**
  - Ensures the efficient utilization of resources in various forms, leading to the creation of necessary economic and social benefits on a sustainable basis.
  - Promotes the fair allocation of benefits, considering the interests of all stakeholders, to prevent any party from benefiting at the expense of others.

- Accounts for the environmental dimension, ensuring that company activities do not have adverse effects on the natural environment.

- **Ethical Responsibility:**
  - Upholds ethical organizational behavior based on principles of fairness honesty, transparency, and responsible dealings.
  - Emphasizes the integrity of transactions between management and stakeholders.

In essence, the importance of governance lies in facilitating the realization of the sustainable development concept, which entails meeting present needs without jeopardizing the ability of future generations to meet their own needs. Governance plays a pivotal role in maximizing economic performance while also taking into account social and environmental considerations within an ethical framework. This alignment with the sustainable development concept involves reconciling environmental, economic, and social development objectives. It involves respecting natural ecosystems, supporting life on Earth, ensuring economic viability without overlooking social goals such as poverty reduction and unemployment alleviation and striving for fairness.

3. Corporate Governance Values

Corporate governance values are fundamental principles and standards established within an organization to guide ethical actions and practices. These values serve as guidelines for evaluating the conduct of individuals and the organization as a whole. They hold significant power and influence within the organization, stemming from a commitment to uphold them universally. Any deviation from these values represents a departure from the organization's objectives and can undermine its integrity and effectiveness. Therefore, adherence to corporate governance values is essential for maintaining trust, accountability, and sustainability within the organization.

- **Importance of the Corporate Value Framework**

The value framework serves as an indicator and conclusive evidence of the organization's progress and advancement. It provides a clear roadmap for assessing the organization's performance and determining its alignment with its overarching goals and objectives.

Activating the value framework is one of the most crucial elements for achieving efficient and effective use of the organization's available resources. By adhering to the established values, the organization can optimize resource allocation and streamline operations to maximize productivity and performance.

Values represent an essential element in any organization as they provide a basis for understanding attitudes, motivation, and influencing individuals' attitudes and behaviors. By promoting a culture that prioritizes and embodies these values, organizations can foster a positive work environment, enhance employee engagement, and promote ethical decision-making at all levels.

The governance concept itself is based on a set of core values, driving management to ensure the achievement of those values to ultimately secure stakeholders' interests. By upholding these values, organizations can enhance trust and confidence among stakeholders, mitigate risks, and sustain long-term success and sustainability. These values originate from various sources, including:

- **Religious beliefs:** Values rooted in religious teachings and beliefs may influence organizational culture and decision-making processes.
- **Social values and ethics**: Societal norms, values, and ethical standards shape organizational behavior and guide interactions with stakeholders.
- **Family values and ethics of the company's employees**: The personal values and ethics of employees, influenced by their upbringing and personal experiences, contribute to the organizational culture.
- **Legislation and laws**: Legal requirements and regulations set by government authorities establish standards for corporate behavior and governance practices.

- **The company's instructions and regulations**: Internal policies guidelines, and codes of conduct established by the organization outline expected behaviors and standards of conduct for employees.

In the corporate governance area, the OECD Principles of Corporate Governance stand out as a primary source of those values. These principles have been formulated to ensure the realization of core values such as transparency, accountability, and fairness. They provide a framework for guiding corporate governance practices and promoting responsible corporate behavior. Adhering to these principles helps organizations uphold integrity, build trust with stakeholders, and achieve sustainable long-term success.

3.1 Transparency

According to Fung (2014), transparency refers to the extent to which an organization's actions are clear and visible to outside parties.

Florini (2007) defines transparency as "the degree to which information is available to outsiders that enables them to have informed voice in decisions and/or assess the decisions made by insiders".

Bushman et al. (2004) define transparency "as the availability of firm specific information to those outside publicly traded firms."

Valletta (2005) defines transparency as accounting disclosure that goes beyond generally accepted accounting principles, standards and legislative requirements in the financial report to provide users with the information they need to make decisions

From these definitions, it is evident that:

- The concept of transparency is diametrically opposed to confidentiality, ambiguity, or lack of clarity. It advocates for openness and accessibility of information.

- Transparency is closely associated with the disclosure of high-quality financial and non-financial information, emphasizing the importance of providing comprehensive and reliable data.
- Transparency entails disclosing more information than what is legally mandated, going beyond minimum requirements to offer a complete understanding of the organization's operations and performance.
- The primary objective of transparency is to cater to the information needs of users, ensuring that they have access to relevant and reliable data to make informed decisions.

While some accounting literature may equate transparency with full disclosure, this perspective overlooks the varying informational requirements of different stakeholders. Simply providing all available information may not adequately meet the diverse needs of stakeholders, highlighting the importance of tailoring transparency efforts to address specific user needs.

On the other hand, the principles of corporate governance emphasized transparency, with a separate principle devoted to it. The other principles also underscored the importance of transparency, given the significant role it played in the financial collapses and crises that affected the world.

For instance, in the case of Enron, the fundamental issue was not solely the mandatory disclosure system itself but rather the market's failure to adequately interpret the available information. Enron's complex financial structures and transactions were often obscured in dense financial reports, making it challenging for investors to discern the company's true financial health. Consequently, the current emphasis is on ensuring that investors have unfettered access to all pertinent information necessary to make well-informed decisions.

Accordingly, governments and international organizations have urgently advocated for applying corporate governance concepts to prevent such crises and collapses, safeguarding stakeholder rights and the company survival and continuity. Since these preceding events showed a crisis of confidence, corporate governance principles have included an emphasis on disclosure and transparency, considering transparency as one of seven criteria for evaluating good corporate governance.

To ensure transparency, governance principles have required several procedures that management must adhere to, including compliance with laws and regulations, utilization of high-quality accounting standards, external audits, stakeholder engagement, and recognition of stakeholders' rights. The board of directors plays a pivotal role in guiding, supervising, and controlling executive management practices and accountability. Additionally, the board is accountable to stakeholders for all organizational procedures and operations.

Based on the above, and since corporate governance aims to protect the interests of stakeholders, the concept of corporate governance is based on the concern to achieve transparency, as transparency enables stakeholders to rationalize their decisions and thus protect their interests.

3.1. Accountability

Transparency is not an end in itself, but rather a way to remove confusion and achieve clarity. However, transparency alone may lose its effectiveness and become ineffectual unless it is coupled with the organization's accountability for its actions. Without stakeholders actively seeking information and explanations regarding the organization's activities, achieving transparency holds little value. Similarly, accountability cannot be enforced without first achieving transparency. Matters that remain undisclosed cannot be subject to discussion, making it exceedingly challenging to hold individuals or entities accountable.

Transparency enhances accountability by enabling effective monitoring, while accountability, in turn, enhances transparency by incentivizing agents to clarify their actions. Both transparency and accountability impose rigor, thereby enhancing the quality of the decision-making process.

The United Nations Development Programme (UNDP) (2008) defines accountability as the obligation to demonstrate that work is conducted according to agreed rules and standards, and to fairly and accurately report on performance relative to roles or plans. This involves transparency, adherence to standards, and responsibility for results. According to Gray et al. (1996) Accountability refers to "the duty to provide an account (by no means necessarily a financial account) or reckoning of those actions for which one is held responsible". This includes corporate social reporting as a means to communicate with various stakeholders.

Ebrahim (2003) perceives accountability as "the means through which individuals and organizations are held externally to account for their actions and as the means by which they take internal responsibility for continuously shaping and scrutinizing organizational mission, goals, and performance". Keasey and Wright (1993) posit that accountability is a component of governance, encompassing the monitoring, evaluation, and oversight of agents to ensure their actions align with the best interests of shareholders and other stakeholders.

These definitions consider accountability as the organization's capacity to respond to the inquiries or apprehensions of stakeholders, or as a portrayal of an action leading to management fulfilling its obligations towards its stakeholders. Consequently, accountability can be viewed as embodying the entitlement of stakeholders to understand the degree to which management adheres to the terms of the contract governing their association. This entitlement to knowledge emanates from the crucial resources bestowed by stakeholders upon the company to execute its operations. The necessity for accountability emerges from the divergence of interests stemming from information asymmetry and conflicts of interests between stakeholders.

Accountability assumes a crucial role in mitigating information asymmetry between management and stakeholders. It serves as a mechanism to regulate agency costs, as companies with lower levels of accountability tend to prioritize the interests of management over those of stakeholders. Any governance mechanism is rendered ineffective without management's accountability. As governance mechanisms are designed to ensure effective management of the company, every aspect of the organization should incorporate mechanisms not only for the efficient utilization of resources but also for ensuring accountability in their utilization.

The above emphasizes the significance of accountability in the governance system, as a fundamental component to attain the safeguarding of stakeholders' interests. Efficiency in the utilization of resources is insufficient to evaluate the effectiveness of management, unless the latter is accompanied by the necessary knowledge of how those resources have been exploited. The company may achieve substantial financial results, but in order to reach this, it may have caused damage to the surrounding environment. In the absence of accountability, there may be a lack of appropriate objectives, and the organization may be deemed efficient irrespective of the methods employed to achieve those results.

One of the basic tools for achieving accountability is disclosure. Disclosure essentially provides answers about what happened, how it happened, and why it happened. The nature of news (informational) and dialogue disclosure through information can be considered as a basis for managing the relationship between the company and its stakeholders. The means of management in this regard is various forms of reporting. It helps the management to offer official explanations about its practices. Therefore, the reports published by the company are considered the foundation for achieving accountability.

The principles of governance reinforce this notion by stipulating a series of procedures to be adhered to in this context. These procedures include ensuring the company's management complies with laws and regulations, adheres to high-quality accounting standards, undergoes independent review, engages stakeholders, and recognizes their rights. The Board of Directors is tasked with guiding, supervising, and controlling executive management practices and ensuring their accountability. Additionally, the board is accountable to stakeholders for all of the company's practices

The primary aim of corporate governance is to safeguard the interests of all stakeholders associated with the organization, including shareholders, employees, suppliers, and the community. A crucial aspect of effective corporate governance is the emphasis on fostering accountability. Accountability enables stakeholders to assess and monitor the trends and practices of the company's management team. By giving prominence to accountability, the entire corporate governance system becomes more transparent and better equipped to address the needs of all stakeholders.

3.2. Fairness

According to Al-Isfahani (as cited in Al-Lawzi, 2014), fairness lies in the middle of all its extremities, with unfairness being a deviation from the middle either through excess or deficiency, and therefore unfairness and error are the opposites of fairness and correctness, which are infinite good. In Aristotle's view, fairness aims to give everyone what he deserves.

Al-Lawzi (2014) pointed out that there is no comprehensive and anti-fairness definition, and that most of what has been mentioned about fairness are descriptions of the achievement of fairness. This researcher collected these descriptions as follows:

- **Moderation and equality between all parties:** Fairness entails ensuring that each party is treated equitably, without unfair treatment to any.
- **Practical application principle:** Fairness is best understood through its practical implementation. It's not just a theoretical concept but is realized through actions and decisions.
- **Absence of unfairness and imbalance:** Fairness is characterized by the absence of unfair treatment and a balance in the interests of all parties involved.

The descriptions of fairness provided by Al-Lawzi (2014) are largely consistent with the foundational principles of corporate governance. Governance is grounded in the equitable treatment of all stakeholders, respecting their rights, balancing their varied interests, and protecting them from harm. In this way, governance provides a practical philosophical and methodological framework to achieve these objectives. Rather than solely conceptualizing ideals or providing general guidance, governance emphasizes the concrete implementation of the underlying principles and values. This transition moves beyond abstract descriptions toward practical enactment

It's essential to highlight that the envisioned equality in governance is grounded in fairness rather than absolute uniformity. Stakeholders may vary in the rights and resources they bring to the company, and genuine fairness necessitates recognizing these differences. If governance mandated total equality irrespective of stakeholder roles and contributions, it would, in reality, distort the concept of fairness.

The principle of equal treatment of shareholders within corporate governance does not imply absolute equality, but rather ensures that all shareholders can exercise the full scope of rights they are entitled to without discrimination. As explained by the OECD (2004), this equates shareholders in terms of the right to participate and vote in general assemblies, while differentiation occurs in the weighting of those votes based on the number of shares held.

A shareholder, whether they hold a significant or minor stake, is regarded as an owner of the corporation. However, the level of resources and risks they have contributed to the organization may differ depending on the size of their shareholding. Therefore, as owners, all shareholders possess the fundamental right to vote. However, the influence or impact of their vote is proportionate to the extent of risk and resources they have invested.

If there had been an arrangement to grant equal voting rights regardless of the size of shareholdings, it would have amounted to a departure from genuine fairness. Such a decision would have posed significant adverse consequences for the sustainability and operation of the company. Corporate governance acknowledges that equitable treatment does not require absolute parity, but rather fair consideration of the distinct roles, risks, and contributions of each shareholder.

By adhering to the principle of "one vote per share," governance guarantees that the voting rights of shareholders correspond to the substantial ownership and risk exposure they possess in the corporation. This reflects the implementation of fairness-driven principles in practice, sidestepping the drawbacks of imposing uniform equality among stakeholders with varying stakes in the organization.

The principles of corporate governance broaden the acknowledgment of fairness beyond shareholders to encompass all pertinent stakeholders. Similar to shareholders who contribute resources and bear risks, other stakeholders like employees, suppliers, and the community also play vital roles in the company through their diverse contributions. Disregarding the legitimate rights of these stakeholders would amount to an unfair and unjust practice.

Governance frameworks underscore the importance of recognizing the established rights of all stakeholders, offering them channels for recourse if their rights are infringed upon. This entails involving stakeholders in the governance process, guaranteeing timely and sufficient access to pertinent information, and empowering them to raise concerns regarding any unethical or illegal activities.

Achieving fairness necessitates striking a balance between the varied interests of shareholders and other stakeholders. Any agreement or compromise between these groups that does not adequately mirror their respective contributions and risk exposures would be inherently unjust. The response to stakeholder interests should be calibrated based on the nature and extent of the resources they have contributed to the organization.

It would be unjust and counterproductive for a business entity focused on profit to become overly charitable at the expense of its owners. Conversely, it would also be unjust and unethical for the organization to become destructive towards society and the environment. Governance must strike a careful balance to uphold the legitimate rights and interests of all affected parties.

The concept of fairness in this context encompasses both distributive and reciprocal forms. Reciprocal fairness pertains to the balance and exchange within contractual relationships, where each party has obtained the intended benefits. This extends beyond just contractual obligations, as the principle of reciprocity also requires those who cause harm to make amends and provide compensation. Upholding these dual dimensions of fairness is crucial for effective and ethical corporate governance. Governance is built upon reciprocal fairness, as the governance system integrates the inputs of contractual clauses, and its outcomes align with the objectives of those clauses. The principles of governance also obligate the Board of Directors to prioritize the interests of stakeholders in instances of illegal or unethical practices and acknowledge their entitlement to compensation if their interests suffer harm. Furthermore, equality or compromise, as demonstrated previously, isn't inherent in governance, as it necessitates a harmonization of interests and, consequently, benefits.

Regarding equitable distribution, it's noted that it revolves around allocating equal shares to the collective body of individuals as members, ensuring each person enjoys the advantages of the common good. While fairness in this context is rooted in equality, it's not purely arithmetic. Equitable distribution requires that allocations among individuals correspond proportionally to their assets, capabilities, and necessities. This embodies a form of proportional equality, aligning with the capacity of each member of society, their standing, and the value of their contributions to society.

It can also be stated that governance is founded on the equitable distribution of benefits and burdens. If we view the company as representing the collective group and individuals as stakeholders, we observe that governance embraces the principle of equitable distribution. This is because it acknowledges the necessity of allocating outcomes proportionally, taking into account the relative significance and requirements of each stakeholder.

CHAPTER 2
THEORIES OF CORPORATE GOVERNANCE

Chapter 2: Theories of Corporate Governance

In this chapter, we embark on an exploration of explanatory theories within the domain of corporate governance. Specifically, our focus lies on the interpretative framework encapsulated by agency theory and stakeholder theory, which have attracted widespread acceptance among researchers and scholars alike. These theories provide valuable insights into the intricate dynamics of governance within organizations, elucidating the relationships between principals, such as shareholders, and agents, such as managers, while also considering the broader network of stakeholders affected by corporate decisions.

1. Agency theory

Agency theory posits organizations as structured around explicit and implicit contractual agency relationships among parties with conflicting interests. Jensen and Meckling (1976) delineate the agency relationship as a contract wherein a principal delegates certain services, including decision-making authority, to an agent. This framework chiefly examines the interplay between shareholders, acting as the principal party, and management, serving as the agent party, within the institutional context. It highlights inherent conflicts of interest inherent in such relationships, elucidating their impact on managerial decision-making processes and organizational performance.

The foundational premise of agency theory rests on the assumption that both parties involved in the relationship are rational and self-interested, thereby striving to maximize their individual benefits. Consequently, this sets the stage for a potential conflict of interest between them. Within the framework of agency theory and considering the segregation of ownership from management, the agent possesses the capacity to access information inaccessible to the principal, resulting in what is termed as information asymmetry. This information asymmetry presents challenges for the principal in effectively monitoring the behavior of the agent.

The accounting literature extensively illustrates that the separation of ownership from management, along with the differing interests of the agent and the principal, gives rise to issues of moral hazard and conflicting choices. Moral hazard refers to situations where the principal incurs losses due to the ethical lapses or actions of the agent, who may not exert sufficient effort to maximize the principal's returns. This occurs because the principal lacks direct control mechanisms to assess the agent's efforts, and the agent is the primary source of information. The second issue arises from disparities in the quantity and quality of information available to both parties. In cases where the principal cannot directly observe the agent's performance or verify the outcomes of their decisions, the principal faces challenges in determining whether the agent has selected the most appropriate course of action.

Henceforth, and with some degree of simplification, within the framework of ownership separate from management, an agency conflict arises from the divergent interests inherent in the contractual relationship. This conflict epitomizes the challenges of agency stemming from the inherent delegation of decision-making authority to the agent acting on behalf of the principal. Management, vested with the authority to utilize resources, possesses comprehensive information pertinent to the organization. Conversely, owners serve as the source and proprietors of these resources. In addition to their authority to appoint managers, owners require information for performance evaluation purposes. Consequently, an information asymmetry prevails in terms of both quantity and type between the two parties involved in the contract. In addition to the information asymmetry, both parties involved in the contract are inclined to focus their endeavors on maximizing their respective benefits. However, these benefits may not align entirely, thus giving rise to a degree of conflict or divergence of interests. Consequently, the agent (management), driven by the pursuit of maximizing their own benefit and leveraging their informational advantage, may exploit the principal's (owners') inability to monitor their actions closely. This allows the agent to make decisions that prioritize their own benefit, rather than necessarily aligning with the interests of the principal. In response, the principal (owners) endeavors to monitor the agent's (management's) actions and incentivize decisions that serve the principal's interests.

In conjunction with the aforementioned dynamics, to mitigate the challenges of agency inherent in contractual relationships, the organization incurs additional expenses termed as agency costs. As stated by Al.Shirazi (1991) these costs encompass:

- **Residual loss:** characterized by the adverse impact on share and bond prices stemming from the likelihood of agent decisions conflicting with the principal's interests.
- **Commitment costs:** which entail expenditures incurred by the agent to reassure and build trust with the principal, thereby safeguarding the principal's interests.
- **Supervision and oversight costs:** encompassing the expenses borne by the principal to monitor and oversee the actions of the agent, ensuring alignment with the principal's objectives.

In essence, these costs are incurred by the agency and represent the embodiment of procedures aimed at ensuring that management acts in the best interests of shareholders or lenders. They essentially embody governance procedures or mechanisms utilized to mitigate the opportunistic behavior of management. In other words, agency theory advocates for the establishment of governance structures to counteract management's opportunistic behavior through the implementation of a set of legal contracts aimed at monitoring management's actions. This may include initiatives such as reducing the number of executive members within the board of directors to enhance its independence, establishing specialized board committees, implementing an internal control system, and designing reward and incentive systems tied to financial performance to incentivize management to enhance its performance.

2. Stakeholder theory

Stakeholder theory is founded on the fundamental premise that the conduct of diverse stakeholders shapes management's responsiveness to the organization's environment. This theory revolves around the interactions between the organization and its external milieu, examining the reactions elicited from stakeholders. Freeman (1984) delineates stakeholders as "any individual or group that can influence or is influenced by the actions, decisions, policies, practices, or objectives of the organization," encompassing, though not limited to, shareholders, suppliers, consumers, customers, employees, governments, local communities. According to this theory, a social contract exists between the organization and each stakeholder, affording them the entitlement to receive benefits and access to information concerning the organization's impacts on them.
Numerous researchers have endeavored to devise classifications of stakeholders. Some propose a division into primary and secondary stakeholders, while others advocate for an internal versus external classification.

- **Primary vs. Secondary Stakeholders**
  - **Primary stakeholders:** These are individuals or groups directly impacted by the organization's actions, decisions, or outcomes. They typically have a significant financial or operational interest in the organization. Examples include shareholders, employees, customers, suppliers, and local communities.
  - **Secondary stakeholders:** These stakeholders are indirectly affected by the organization and may have less influence or involvement compared to primary stakeholders. They might include government agencies, regulatory bodies, media, competitors, and special interest groups.
- **Internal vs. External Stakeholders**

- **Internal stakeholders:** These are individuals or groups directly associated with the organization and typically have a formal relationship with it. They may include employees, managers, executives, and shareholders.
  - **External stakeholders:** These stakeholders have an interest in the organization but are not directly involved in its day-to-day operations. They can include customers, suppliers, local communities, government agencies, advocacy groups, and competitors.

Furthermore, alternative classifications have been suggested, reflecting differing interpretations of stakeholders' significance and roles within organizational contexts. These classifications may encompass various criteria such as their level of influence, proximity to the organization, or degree of involvement in its activities.

- **Level of Influence**
  - **Key stakeholders:** These are individuals or groups with significant influence over the organization's decisions, actions, or outcomes. They often have the power to shape the organization's strategies and goals.
  - **Marginal stakeholders:** These stakeholders have limited influence or importance to the organization and may be less prioritized in stakeholder management efforts.
- **Proximity to the Organization**
  - **Close stakeholders:** These are stakeholders with a close relationship or direct interaction with the organization. They may have a vested interest in its success or failure due to their close ties.
  - **Distant stakeholders:** These stakeholders have a more distant or indirect relationship with the organization and may be less directly impacted by its actions.
- **Degree of Involvement**
  - **Active stakeholders:** These stakeholders actively participate in the organization's activities, engage in dialogue, and contribute to decision-making processes.

- **Passive stakeholders:** These stakeholders have an interest in the organization but are less actively involved in its operations or decision-making processes.

▪ **Salience or Relevance**

- **Critical stakeholders:** These stakeholders are deemed essential to the organization's success or survival due to their significant impact or dependence on the organization.
- **Non-critical stakeholders:** These stakeholders may have less immediate importance or impact on the organization's operations or objectives.

Ultimately, the classification of stakeholders is contingent upon researchers' conceptualizations of stakeholder theory and their objectives in analyzing stakeholder dynamics within organizations.

The application of stakeholder theory is often fraught with challenges and characterized by ambiguity due to several factors. Primarily, one significant challenge lies in the identification of stakeholders and their evolving needs. Stakeholders can vary in nature and may include individuals, groups, or entities with diverse interests and perspectives. Moreover, stakeholders' needs and priorities are subject to constant change, further complicating the task of accurately identifying and addressing them. This dynamic nature of stakeholders and their needs necessitates continuous monitoring and adaptation by organizations.

Additionally, the process of identifying stakeholders and understanding their needs entails significant costs for organizations. Resources must be allocated to conduct comprehensive stakeholder analyses, gather relevant data, and develop strategies to engage with stakeholders effectively. Furthermore, organizations must invest in ongoing communication and relationship-building efforts to maintain a thorough understanding of stakeholder concerns and preferences.

Stakeholder theory triggers a wide-ranging debate regarding whether organizations should consider all stakeholder interests indiscriminately, or prioritize the interests of certain parties over others. This debate revolves around the ethical and practical implications of stakeholder management and the extent to which organizations should balance competing interests.

2.1. The normative perspective

The normative perspective of stakeholder theory advocates for organizations to respond to all stakeholders' interests impartially, irrespective of their relative importance or influence. This ethical framework emphasizes an obligation to address the concerns of all stakeholders equally, guided by philosophical principles. In adhering to this perspective, organizations extend their responsiveness to encompass non-traditional stakeholders, thereby fulfilling their moral duties as outlined by the social contract.

However, this perspective disregards the practical complexities of stakeholder management. It fails to account for the varying degrees of influence wielded by different stakeholders, potentially resulting in inefficiencies or conflicts in governance practices. Despite its idealistic aspirations, the normative perspective primarily outlines prescriptive guidelines for organizational conduct, rather than reflecting the nuanced realities of stakeholder engagement. Consequently, scholars have proposed an alternative viewpoint termed the administrative perspective.

2.2. The managerial perspective

The managerial perspective, derived from empirical studies, adopts a pragmatic approach towards stakeholder theory. Advocates of this perspective recognize the varying degrees of influence among stakeholders and acknowledge that organizations may prioritize responses to stakeholders based on their relative importance. Consequently, the company's actions in addressing stakeholder interests are tailored to reflect the significance of each stakeholder.

In practice, this approach necessitates the balancing of stakeholder interests within the organization. By addressing the diverse needs and demands of stakeholders, organizations can align their long-term goals with the interests of key stakeholders. This balanced approach acknowledges the importance of stakeholder management in organizational decision-making processes and aims to foster mutually beneficial relationships with stakeholders.

The relationship between a company and its stakeholders is often viewed as reciprocal in nature. Shareholders, for instance, provide capital to the company and expect returns on their investment in the form of profits. Similarly, lenders extend funding to the company and anticipate timely repayment of their dues. Customers engage with the company by purchasing its products, expecting high-quality offerings at reasonable prices in return.

Additionally, local communities and society at large provide the company with the necessary infrastructure and environment to conduct its operations. In exchange, they expect the company to exhibit good citizenship and social responsibility, ensuring that its activities do not detrimentally impact the quality of life within society.

This reciprocal relationship underscores the interdependence between the company and its stakeholders, highlighting the mutual expectations and obligations that shape their interactions. By fulfilling its responsibilities towards stakeholders, the company can cultivate trust, goodwill, and long-term sustainability within its operating environment.

As previously highlighted, the normative perspective suggesting that a company is accountable to all stakeholders ultimately renders it accountable to none. Likewise, the managerial perspective, which advocates for balancing stakeholder needs, primarily emphasizes how stakeholders can safeguard their interests but does not explore the mechanisms through which they can achieve this protection. Consequently, an alternative viewpoint emerges: the agency perspective of stakeholders.

2.3. The Stakeholder-Agency Theory by Hill and Jones (1992)

The Stakeholder-Agency Theory integrates two distinct theoretical frameworks: stakeholder theory and agency theory. Stakeholder theory focuses on how organizations address the needs and concerns of their various stakeholders. In contrast, agency theory examines the supervisory and motivational mechanisms within the relationship between an agent and a principal. This relationship is often characterized by conflicts of interest stemming from the self-interested behavior of both parties involved in the contractual arrangement. By merging these two perspectives, the Stakeholder-Agency Theory provides insights into how organizations navigate the complex dynamics of stakeholder relationships while also addressing the challenges posed by agency conflicts.

This perspective regards the company as a network of contracts established among various stakeholders, who are the owners of resources. It broadens the management's role beyond solely safeguarding the interests of shareholders to also encompass preserving the interests of other stakeholders within the organization.

According to Hill and Jones (1992), stakeholders encompass all groups that possess a legitimate claim or entitlement to the organization. This legitimacy is established through an exchange relationship, wherein each group provides the company with essential resources required to conduct its operations. In return, each group expects the company to address its interests and concerns. The researchers further identify stakeholders as shareholders, lenders, management, employees, customers, suppliers, local communities, and society at large, based on their involvement in this exchange relationship.

Additionally, Hill and Jones (1992) underscore that the management occupies a central position within the contracting network that forms the foundation of the organization. It is the sole stakeholder that engages in contractual relationships with all other stakeholders and possesses direct decision-making authority. Consequently, management is obligated to consider the rights of stakeholders when formulating strategic decisions and allocating the organization's resources.

In this theory, it is emphasized that the majority of relationships between stakeholders and management are governed by implicit contracts. Stakeholder implicitly expect the company to fulfill their demands in exchange for providing resources. To ensure the fulfillment of these expectations, a variety of institutional structures are employed to monitor and enforce these implicit agreements.

Moreover, given the interconnection between the company's operations and the resources provided by stakeholders, and the distinct position of management relative to them, management assumes the role of an agent for all stakeholders. In this context, the original agent relationship, upon which agency theory is founded, can be viewed as part of a broader relationship between management and stakeholders within the company. According to Hill and Jones (1992), both relationships involve implicit or explicit contracts and are subject to supervision through a set of control mechanisms. The researchers further assert that many principles and concepts derived from agency theory can be applied to the relationship between management and stakeholders.

According to Hill and Jones (1992), acknowledging that the remaining stakeholders hold demands and rights within the company, it is evident that prioritizing their needs will likely result in a reduction of the benefits achievable by the management compared to pursuing their own interests. Workers aim for safe and favorable working conditions, customers seek access to high-quality products, while local communities and society at large aspire to minimize environmental pollution levels. Undoubtedly, addressing these demands will likely result in a decrease in profits for the management. This scenario can potentially give rise to conflicts of interest due to information asymmetry and differing interests among stakeholders. Consequently, such conflicts may lead to the occurrence of what is termed as "forgone benefits." This concept reflects the disparity between the benefits that stakeholders could have realized if the management had acted in their best interests versus the benefits obtained when the management prioritizes its self-interest. As a result, stakeholders may bear the costs associated with contracting, including agency costs, in an effort to mitigate these forgone benefits. These costs stem from stakeholders' utilization of institutional structures aimed at monitoring and effectively implementing contracts to curtail the management's capacity for self-interested behavior to the detriment of stakeholders' interests. These structures aid in mitigating information asymmetry by reducing the costs associated with information retrieval. Additionally, they enable stakeholders to exert pressure on the management to adopt behaviors that align with the interests of all parties involved.

As outlined by Hill and Jones (1992), these institutional structures manifest in reconciliatory, control, and support mechanisms.

- **Reconciliatory mechanisms** include pre-established agreements such as product warranties.
- **As for control mechanisms,** they play a crucial role in mitigating the issue of information asymmetry. Due to their limited access to information, stakeholders may incur significant costs in searching for, gathering, and analyzing information, which may be prohibitive for some stakeholders. Therefore, the significance of control mechanisms, as highlighted by Hill and Jones, becomes apparent. These mechanisms include:

- Legal requirements, such as mandatory annual reporting obligations, which compel organizations to disclose essential information to stakeholders.
- Information services provided by entities such as financial analysts, which offer stakeholders access to expert analysis and insights.
- Non-profit organizations, such as environmental groups and labor unions, which advocate for stakeholder interests and provide information and support on relevant issues.

- **Support mechanisms** complement control mechanisms and play a crucial role in discouraging management from prioritizing its interests over those of stakeholders. As noted by Hill and Jones (1992):

- Legislation serves as a deterrent by enabling the imposition of sanctions on the management for non-compliance.
- Deviation from contractual relationships is effective through the presence of federations or bodies representing stakeholders, such as trade unions or

consumer federations, which have the potential to initiate strikes or boycotts of the company's products.

- Publicity allows stakeholders to engage in anti-establishment propaganda, leading to reputational damage for the company.

From the foregoing, it can be inferred that this perspective redefines the notion of institutional responsibility. In this view, management is not simply an agent of one party, namely the owners, but rather an agent of a collective of stakeholders, which encompasses not only owners but also other parties with legitimate demands based on the resources they provide to the company. This perspective advocates for an expansion of the contractual relationship upon which the company operates, as well as an expanded role for management. Rather than solely focusing on maximizing profits for the benefit of shareholders, management is expected to consider the needs of all stakeholders, including broader societal concerns. It is recognized that the survival and sustainability of the company hinge on achieving both economic and non-economic objectives, which can only be accomplished by addressing the diverse needs of stakeholders. In essence, this perspective contends that safeguarding the interests of each party with resources in the company necessitates taking into account the interests of all other parties.

With critical analysis, it becomes evident that managers often prioritize projects with immediate financial gains or quick returns on investment, potentially delaying investments in long-term beneficial projects. Additionally, focusing on social and environmental considerations can incur substantial costs for the company, with financial benefits typically realized over the medium to long term.

From the management's perspective, prioritizing environmental and social aspects may seem counterintuitive as it could divert resources away from endeavors that maximize self-interest. Conversely, stakeholders prioritize social and environmental issues as these directly impact their interests in the company. However, stakeholders face challenges in ensuring that their resources are allocated in a manner consistent with their interests, especially considering the asymmetry of information between management and stakeholders.

This information asymmetry fuels conflicts of interest between management and stakeholders within the company. Consequently, stakeholders bear the initial costs of contracting. To mitigate these costs, stakeholders employ governance mechanisms, including internal measures such as the Board of Directors and external measures such as legislation and financial market regulations. These mechanisms aim to ensure that management acts in the best interests of stakeholders and the company as a whole.

3. Managerial entrenchment theory

The managerial entrenchment theory, within its conceptual framework, extends from both agency theory and transaction costs theory. It emphasizes the necessity of establishing control mechanisms to delineate boundaries, particularly addressing the risk of CEO entrenchment and the challenges posed by information asymmetry between contractual parties, which impact the company's performance.
The concept of "entrenchment" suggests that the manager is exerting efforts to solidify their position without risking destabilization, aiming to safeguard their tenure and pursue personal interests. Entrenchment is typically understood as a relational circumstance, whether formal or informal, wherein the CEO seeks to diminish or eliminate even partial control exerted by the Board of Directors and shareholders. This is undertaken to maintain their position, increase autonomy and authority, and optimize personal benefits without opposition.
This theory posits that individuals within the company continuously devise strategies and tactics to fortify their positions within the organizational hierarchy. They strive to impede potential rivals from gaining access to their positions, thereby bolstering their authority and knowledge of internal affairs. However, these strategies may incur costs for the company, including heightened authority and influence of the CEO, who may reap benefits such as rewards and job security. Consequently, most scholars contend that the outcomes of managerial entrenchment represent products of illegitimate authority rather than democratic

processes, conflicting with shareholder interests and detrimentally impacting institutional performance.

According to Shleifer and Vishny (1997), the entrenchment process involves managers making private investments, prioritizing projects aligned with their expertise or experience, even if these projects aren't inherently beneficial for the company. These projects are chosen to ensure the manager's prolonged tenure at the helm of the organization, with the manager potentially receiving additional benefits such as increased compensation, making it challenging for the organization to replace them with another manager.

Hence, the entrenchment theory emphasizes the necessity of activating control mechanisms, recognizing that managerial entrenchment arises in response to internal and external controls aimed at managers.

4. Transaction Cost Theory

This theory is grounded in the notion that the company maintains various internal agreements (regulated) and external agreements (market-driven) to enhance value creation. Each internal agreement within the company incurs transaction costs. When the transaction costs linked to utilizing external markets exceed those of internal transactions, the company opts to conduct the transaction internally, thereby seeking to fulfill it from within.

The American scholar Coase is credited with pioneering this theory in 1937 through his article titled "The Nature of the Firm." In this seminal work, Coase engaged in inquiries concerning the rationale behind the existence of companies, the distinctive factors elucidating variations in their organizational structures, and why companies opt to internalize certain productive activities rather than relying solely on the market to procure the goods and services they require, under the presumption that the market can efficiently coordinate economic activities through price mechanisms.

Coase addressed these inquiries through what he termed transaction costs, positing that these costs serve as a rationale for the existence of companies. Companies emerge as a substitute for more costly transaction methods, acting as intermediaries to streamline transactions between service seekers and providers. Coase suggests that it is the organizational labor relations that facilitate this streamlining, with the role of workers in this process contingent upon the operational framework, incentives, promotions, and performance monitoring and evaluation. These costs can be categorized into:

- **Cost of information search:** This encompasses expenses associated with seeking out the necessary goods or services, including efforts to ascertain availability, pricing, quality, and other pertinent details.
- **Negotiation costs:** These are the expenses incurred in the process of reaching a mutually agreeable and suitable contract, encompassing time spent in negotiations, legal fees, and related expenditures.
- **Commitment and enforcement costs:** This includes the expenses arising from the necessity to ensure that all parties adhere to the terms of the contract, as well as any consequences resulting from non-compliance with these terms. Such costs may involve monitoring activities, legal actions, or other measures to enforce contractual obligations.

Additionally, Williamson's work (1975), building upon Coase's insights, explored deeper into understanding organizational forms aimed at minimizing transaction costs. His analysis was grounded in two fundamental assumptions:

- **Bounded rationality:** Recognizing that human decision-making is constrained by cognitive limitations, bounded rationality suggests that individuals have limited capacity to process and analyze information comprehensively. As a result, actors within organizations may not always make optimal decisions but instead act within the constraints of their cognitive abilities.
- **Opportunism:** Williamson also posited that individuals within transactions are inherently opportunistic, seeking to maximize their own

self-interests. This assumption acknowledges the potential for parties to exploit information asymmetries or engage in opportunistic behavior to gain advantage in contractual relationships.

Therefore, Williamson's analysis (1975) underscores the complexity inherent in contractual relationships, where it's virtually impossible to foresee and account for every potential scenario or outcome. Due to this inherent uncertainty, contractual arrangements often fall short of capturing all contingencies, leaving gaps that may be exploited by opportunistic behavior. To address this challenge, Williamson (1975) advocates for the establishment of robust control and monitoring mechanisms that can adapt to changing circumstances and mitigate risks as they arise. These mechanisms serve as safeguards against potential breaches of trust and opportunistic actions, ensuring that parties are held accountable for their obligations even in uncertain situations.

In essence, Williamson (1975) argues that effective governance structures are essential for navigating the uncertainties and complexities of contractual arrangements. These structures provide a framework for establishing clear rights, responsibilities, and expectations among parties, while also facilitating mechanisms for resolving disputes and enforcing compliance. By instituting such governance mechanisms, contracting parties can mitigate transactional risks and enhance the efficiency and effectiveness of their interactions.

5. The cognitive theory

The previous contractual theories primarily address issues arising from contracts, such as information asymmetry and conflicts of interest. However, they fail to analyze the value creation process within companies. Instead, their focus remains on the distribution of value. As a result, these theories overlook critical factors essential for achieving sustainable competitive advantage, including efficiency, knowledge management, innovation, and continuous learning.

In cognitive theory, performance is closely linked to a manager's capacity to envision, grasp, and innovate new productive opportunities, along with their ability to adapt within their environment to reorganize existing processes. The company under this theory, is perceived as a reservoir of knowledge that empowers it to identify fresh opportunities for sustainable value creation, rather than merely a network of established contracts as posited in prior theories. This perspective underscores that value generation hinges largely on the manager's personality competencies, and knack for knowledge creation.

This theory places significant emphasis on the role of intellectual or cognitive capital in value creation. Unlike contractual theories, which focus on aligning the interests of stakeholders and management, cognitive theory suggests that the key challenge lies in coordinating, harmonizing, and qualitatively aligning the cognitive models expected to achieve cognitive adjustments among various stakeholders.

Governance mechanisms within this theory should therefore facilitate management in reporting how it has accomplished its designated objectives. The Board of Directors, as one of the governance mechanisms within this perspective, assumes a cognitive role, serving as a forum for the exchange of ideas and discussions where knowledgeable board members can impact managerial competencies. In this regard, governance mechanisms should provide guidance to the manager and empower them to make decisions that foster value creation through innovation and organizational learning.

Aligned with the above perspective, Charreaux (2002) defines corporate governance within this theoretical framework as "a set of mechanisms that enhance the possibility of creating value through learning and innovation." With some simplification, this theory offers a distinct interpretation of governance mechanisms compared to earlier theories. Instead of primarily addressing conflicts, it sees these mechanisms as playing a proactive role. Thus, it underscores the necessity for the governance system to encompass mechanisms that facilitate optimal opportunities for value creation through learning and innovation.

CHAPTER 3

CORPORATE GOVERNANCE PRINCIPLES AND MECHANISMS

Chapter 3: Corporate Governance Principles and Mechanisms

Corporate governance principles have attracted increasing attention, prompting a range of regional and international bodies to conduct extensive studies and analyses on this subject. These entities aim to establish standards for its implementation and articulate principles intended to serve as fundamental benchmarks for policymakers. Such endeavors seek to evaluate and enhance the legal, institutional, and regulatory frameworks governing corporate governance. Notable contributors to this discourse include the Organization for Economic Cooperation and Development (OECD), the Basel Committee, the World Bank, the International Monetary Fund (IMF), and the Bank for International Settlements (BIS). The works of the OECD and the Basel Committee are particularly noteworthy and widely recognized in this field.

1. The OECD Corporate governance principles

The OECD introduced a comprehensive framework for corporate governance with the release of the OECD Principles on Corporate Governance in 2004. These principles were the culmination of extensive consultations, drawing upon expertise not only from OECD member states but also from countries outside the organization. Additionally, input was solicited from experts worldwide, as well as stakeholders representing various sectors such as federations, unions, and businesses. Oversight of these consultations was provided by the OECD Corporate Governance Leadership Group, with observer participation from esteemed entities including the World Bank, the International Monetary Fund, the Bank for

International Settlements, the Financial Stability Forum, the Basel Committee, and the International Organization of Securities Supervisors (IOSCO).

The International Organization of Securities Supervisors (IOSCO) has emphasized the significance of adhering to these principles, highlighting their role in upholding the integrity of financial markets and bolstering economic stability. Additionally, the OECD underscored that these principles attracted endorsement from the Financial Stability Forum, being recognized as one of the twelve primary standards for sound financial systems. Furthermore, they have served as the cornerstone for the corporate governance component in reports by esteemed institutions such as the World Bank and the International Monetary Fund on the observance of standards and regulations (ROSC).

Since their inception, these principles have served as a benchmark in numerous investor initiatives aimed at crafting guidelines, including the International Corporate Governance Network Guide. They have also influenced the development of guidelines by major investment institutions such as the California Public Employees' Pension Scheme, the Teachers' Association for Insurance and Installment, the Palo MA Retirement Equity Fund, and Hermes Asset Management Company in the United Kingdom. Furthermore, various studies suggest that all the principles, rules, and standards of corporate governance established in Arab countries reaffirm the principles set forth by the OECD.

Below are the OECD principles on corporate governance along with the key issues addressed:

Principle 1: Ensuring an Effective Corporate Governance Framework

Principle 1 focuses on ensuring an effective corporate governance framework. Its objective is to establish a foundation for effective corporate governance. This principle addresses key issues such as encouraging transparency and efficiency in markets, ensuring consistency with the rule of law, and clearly defining the distribution of responsibilities among various entities.

Principle 1 underscores the importance of aligning the corporate governance framework with the external environment surrounding the organisation. A framework that harmonizes well with regulations, laws, legislation, and regulatory bodies is more effective in promoting transparency and efficiency in markets.

Principle 2: Shareholders' Rights

The principle of shareholders' rights underscores the significance of safeguarding fundamental shareholder entitlements. It necessitates ensuring mechanisms for recording ownership transfers, providing timely and regular information, facilitating participation and voting in shareholder meetings, electing directors, and receiving dividends. Additionally, shareholders should have access to adequate information regarding decisions pertaining to significant corporate changes, such as mergers or the sale of substantial company assets, enabling them to understand their rights and available courses of action.

Principle 2 emphasizes the paramount importance of shareholders within the organisation, particularly in comparison to other stakeholders, owing to the nature, potency, and relative significance of the resources they provide. Consequently, the framework must meticulously consider and protect the rights of all shareholders, irrespective of their shareholding proportions in the organisation.

Principle 3: Equal treatment of shareholders

The principle equal treatment of shareholders underscores the imperative of equitable treatment for all shareholders within the corporate governance framework. This principle mandates that all shareholders, including minority and foreign shareholders, should be afforded equal treatment, with every shareholder being provided with the opportunity to seek adequate redress for any infringements upon their rights.

Principle 4: The role of stakeholders in corporate governance

This principle underscores the importance of acknowledging the interests of stakeholders beyond shareholders, such as employees, customers, suppliers, and the broader community. It advocates for a cooperative approach that considers the needs and concerns of all stakeholders, not just those of shareholders, in decision-making processes. This delineation highlights several key aspects:

- **Legal Protection:** The framework should ensure that stakeholders' rights, as protected by law, are upheld.
- **Remedies for Violations:** Stakeholders should have recourse to compensation in case their rights are infringed upon.
- **Engagement Mechanisms:** Mechanisms facilitating stakeholder engagement should be integrated into the corporate governance framework to enhance performance.
- **Access to Information:** Stakeholders should have access to relevant and timely information necessary for informed decision-making.
- **Communication Channels:** Stakeholders should be able to communicate their concerns to the Board of Directors, and their rights should be safeguarded when doing so.

This principle underscores the indispensable role of stakeholders in the organisation's sustainability and longevity. It emphasizes the imperative for their active involvement, signaling that an effective corporate governance framework hinges on such engagement. Moreover, it calls for a departure from unethical practices, advocating instead for the pursuit of institutional sustainability, which inherently involves addressing social and environmental considerations. Thus, adherence to good corporate governance practices necessitates this holistic approach.

Principle 5: Disclosure and Transparency

This principle emphasizes the necessity of disclosing all pertinent information concerning the company accurately, promptly, and comprehensively. This encompasses details regarding the financial status, performance metrics, equity structure, and corporate governance practices. The disclosure should encompass a broad range of information, including but not limited to:

- Financial and operational performance results
- Company objectives
- Major shareholders and their voting rights
- Remuneration policy for key directors and executives
- Information on directors and executives, such as qualifications and independence
- Expected risk factors
- Matters concerning employees and other stakeholders
- Corporate governance structures and policies
- The disclosed information, whether financial or non-financial, should adhere to high accounting quality standards in its preparation and presentation.
- An independent auditor should review the disclosed information to provide objective assurance to the Board of Directors and shareholders regarding the accuracy and reliability of the financial statements.
- Information delivery channels should ensure accessibility to users at the appropriate time and cost-effective manner.

This principle underscores the significance of disclosing and communicating both financial and non-financial information to stakeholders, notably shareholders. Such information should possess the quality and independent assurance necessary to provide a fair and reliable representation of the organisation's performance including how it utilizes the resources provided by stakeholders.

Principle 6: Responsibilities of the Board of Directors

The corporate governance framework should offer strategic directives to guide companies and ensure effective oversight of executive management by the Board of Directors. The Board of Directors should be held accountable by the organisation and shareholders. To achieve this:

- Board members must operate with access to complete information, good intentions, and adherence to applicable regulations, striving to serve the interests of the organisation and its shareholders.
- When the decisions of the Board of Directors lead to disparate impacts on various shareholder groups, the Board should strive for equitable treatment of all shareholders.
- The Board is responsible for ensuring compliance with relevant laws and considering the interests of all stakeholders.
- The Board of Directors should perform fundamental functions that underscore its oversight and monitoring authority over corporate activities, enabling it to conduct objective assessments independent of executive management.

This principle underscores the importance of the separation of powers, advocating for a clear division between supervisory and executive functions. It emphasizes granting supervisory bodies the necessary authority to oversee and monitor executive activities, ensuring both branches are accountable to stakeholders. This arrangement enhances stakeholder protection and promotes transparency and accountability within the organization.

It can be said, that the establishment of these principles aims to protect the interests of stakeholders by holding management accountable for decisions that serve their interests (as stipulated in the responsibilities of the Board of Directors) and ensuring shareholders' rights, equal treatment, and stakeholder engagement. Moreover, transparent disclosure practices prevent misinformation, promoting fairness, transparency, and accountability through the separation of powers. This framework fosters an environment of transparency, accountability, and equity, safeguarding the interests of all involved parties. Adaptation to the company's environment is crucial, and adherence to these principles signifies good corporate governance practice.

It's crucial to recognize that the presence of a comprehensive and efficient governance framework within any country hinges upon the presence of various institutional and legislative structures. Key components include a well-developed legal framework, a robust banking sector, competitive markets, transparent tax systems, and an independent judiciary. These elements collectively contribute to fostering an environment conducive to effective governance practices and sustainable economic development.

Given the diversity of circumstances across different contexts, it's challenging to prescribe a one-size-fits-all model for corporate governance. As a result policymakers and legislators are granted the flexibility to tailor governance principles to the unique characteristics of their respective countries. The OECD underscores that these principles are not prescriptive and do not offer off-the-shelf solutions for national legislators. Instead, they serve as a guiding reference for policymakers to develop and refine corporate governance frameworks that align with their nation's economic, social, legal, and cultural contexts. This approach allows for greater adaptability and customization to meet specific needs and circumstances.

2. The Basel Committee Corporate governance principles

The Basel Committee, formally titled the "Committee on Banking Supervision," consists of central bank governors from ten industrialized nations, along with representatives from Switzerland and Luxembourg. Operating under the auspices of the Bank for International Settlements in Basel, Switzerland, it is tasked with developing and disseminating standards and guidelines for best practices in banking supervision. These standards are influenced and endorsed by various international organizations such as the International Monetary Fund (IMF) and the World Bank. They serve as benchmarks for evaluating the robustness of banking supervisory systems and provide guidance to governments seeking assistance from these organizations. Additionally, the Basel Committee's work is informed by the efforts of the Organization for Economic Cooperation and Development (OECD) and the lessons learned from financial crises, including those in Southeast Asia and elsewhere.

The Basel Committee on Banking Supervision released a guidance document aimed at assisting banks in implementing governance principles. Subsequently, it issued a revised version in 2005, followed by a third iteration in 2006, which incorporated principles specific to governance in banks. These principles are intended to provide a framework for banks to enhance their governance practices, ensuring soundness, transparency, and accountability in their operations. The Basel Committee's guidelines serve as a reference point for banks globally, aiding them in aligning their governance structures with international best practices. These principles of governance in banks can be stated as follows:

Principle 1: Board's Overall Responsibilities

The board of directors holds the ultimate responsibility for the bank's operations, including the approval and oversight of management's implementation of the bank's strategic objectives, governance framework, and corporate culture. This involves:

- **Approval of Strategic Objectives:** The board approves the bank's strategic objectives and ensures that management aligns its actions with these objectives.
- **Governance Framework Oversight:** The board is responsible for overseeing the bank's governance framework, ensuring that it effectively manages risks, complies with regulations, and maintains ethical standards.
- **Organizational Structure:** The board establishes and reviews the bank's organizational structure to ensure efficiency and effectiveness in operations.

- **Duty of Care and Loyalty:** Board members are obligated to exercise their duty of care and loyalty to the bank, acting in its best interests and avoiding conflicts of interest.
- **Related Party Transactions:** The board reviews transactions involving related parties to ensure they are conducted fairly and transparently.
- **Setting the Tone at the Top:** The board sets the tone at the top by fostering a culture of integrity, accountability, and ethical behavior throughout the organization.
- **Risk Governance Framework:** The board oversees the bank's risk governance framework, including reviewing key policies, controls, and defining risk appetite.
- **Risk Management Oversight:** The board ensures the effectiveness of risk management, compliance, and internal audit functions, holding them accountable for their roles in maintaining the bank's safety and soundness.
- **CEO Selection and Oversight:** The board selects the CEO and provides oversight of senior management, ensuring they possess the necessary skills and qualifications to lead the bank effectively.

Principle 2: Board Qualifications and Composition

Board members play a crucial role in overseeing the affairs of the bank, and it is essential that they possess the necessary qualifications and attributes to fulfill their responsibilities effectively. This principle emphasizes the following aspects:

- **Composition:**
  - The board should be composed in a manner that facilitates effective oversight and governance. It should consist of individuals with a diverse range of skills, expertise, and backgrounds.
  - An adequate number of independent directors should be included on the board. An independent director is defined as a non-executive member who

does not hold management responsibilities within the bank and is free from undue influence or conflicts of interest.

- The nomination of board members and succession planning should be handled by the board itself, with consideration given to maintaining a balanced and diverse composition. A nomination committee, comprised of independent directors, may be established to identify and nominate suitable candidates.
- If shareholders have the power to appoint board members, the board should ensure that these individuals understand their duties and responsibilities.
- Induction programs should be provided to new board members to familiarize them with their roles and responsibilities.

▪ **Qualifications:**

- Board members should collectively possess a broad range of knowledge and experience in relevant areas, promoting diversity of perspectives and insights. These areas may include capital markets, financial analysis, risk management, corporate governance, and strategic planning, among others.
- The board should have a reasonable understanding of local, regional, and global economic and market dynamics, as well as the legal and regulatory environment in which the bank operates. International experience, where applicable, should also be considered.
- Individual board members should exhibit attitudes conducive to effective communication, collaboration, and critical debate during decision-making processes, fostering an environment of openness and constructive dialogue.

Principle 3: Board Structure and Practices

The board should establish governance structures and practices tailored to its own operations, ensuring they are followed and periodically reviewed for effectiveness. This includes defining leadership, size, committee usage, and updating rules. Regular assessments of the board, its committees, and individual members should be conducted, and appropriate records maintained. The chairman should be independent or non-executive.

A board may set up specialized committees, whose establishment and mandate are determined by the full board. Factors such as the bank's size, its board, business areas, and risk profile influence the number and nature of these committees. Examples include the Audit, Risk, and Compensation committees. Other specialized committees like Nomination, Human Resources, Governance, Ethics, and Compliance may also be advisable. It's recommended that committee chairs be independent non-executive board members.

- **Audit committee**

An audit committee is deemed necessary for systemically important banks and is highly encouraged for other banks, considering factors such as the organization's size, risk profile, and complexity.

The membership of an audit committee should consist entirely of independent or non-executive board members. Its chair must be independent and not hold the position of the board chair or any other committee chair. Additionally, the committee should include members with expertise in audit practices, financial reporting, and accounting. This committee holds several key responsibilities, including:

- Establishing policies related to internal audit and financial reporting.
- Supervising the financial reporting process.
- Interacting with and overseeing both internal and external auditors.
- Approving or recommending the appointment, remuneration, and dismissal of external auditors.
- Reviewing and endorsing the audit scope and frequency.
- Receiving important audit reports and ensuring timely corrective actions are taken by senior management to address identified issues.
- Overseeing the establishment of accounting policies and practices.
- Reviewing third-party opinions on the design and effectiveness of the overall risk governance framework and internal control system.

- **Risk committee**

The risk committee plays a critical role in overseeing risk management within the organization. Its responsibilities include:

- Discussing all risk strategies and providing recommendations on these strategies and the risk appetite to the board
- Conducting a thorough review of the bank's risk policies at least once a year
- Overseeing management's processes to ensure adherence to the established risk policies.

The risk committee should comprise a majority of independent members, with an independent chair who is not the chair of the board or any other committee. It should also include members with expertise in risk management issues and practices.

- **Compensation committee**

A compensation committee is required for systemically important banks. Its key role is to support the board in overseeing the remuneration system to ensure it aligns with the bank's performance, control environment, and compliance with regulatory and legal requirements.

- **Conflicts of interest**

Conflicts of interest policies should be established and overseen by the board, ensuring transparency and proper disclosure to supervisors.

Principle 4: Senior management

This principle underscores the role of senior management in executing the bank's activities within the parameters set by the board. Senior management, accountable to the board, is tasked with the day-to-day management of the bank in alignment with the board-approved business strategy, risk appetite, remuneration, and other policies.

Principle 5: Governance of group structures

Principle 5 emphasizes that within a group structure, the parent company's board holds ultimate responsibility for the entire group. It is tasked with establishing and maintaining a governance framework suitable for the group's structure, business activities, and associated risks. Both the board and senior management must have a comprehensive understanding of the group's organizational setup and the risks it entails. Additional guidance is offered for boards of subsidiary companies and in cases of complex or opaque group structures.

Principle 6: Risk management function

Principle 6 underscores the necessity for banks to establish a robust independent risk management function, led by a Chief Risk Officer (CRO) possessing adequate authority, autonomy, resources, and direct access to the board. This function serves as a critical component of the bank's second line of defence, tasked with overseeing risk-taking activities. Particularly for large, complex, and internationally active banks, as well as others based on their risk profile and local governance mandates, a senior manager, such as the CRO or equivalent, should be appointed to oversee the bank's risk management function. Any changes to the CRO position, including appointment, dismissal, or other alterations, must receive approval from the board or its designated risk committee. Furthermore, if the CRO is removed from the position, public disclosure should be made, and discussions regarding the reasons for the removal should be held with the bank's supervisor.

Principle 7: Risk identification, monitoring and controlling

Under Principle of the Basel Committee's guidelines, there is a strong emphasis on the ongoing identification, monitoring, and control of risks at both the bank-wide and individual entity levels. This principle underscores the necessity for the bank's risk management and internal control infrastructure to remain adaptable, evolving alongside changes in the bank's risk profile, the external risk environment, and industry standards. Detailed guidance is provided within this principle regarding the processes involved in risk identification, measurement, and management.

Principle 8: Risk communication

This principle highlights the critical importance of robust risk communication within the bank. Effective risk governance hinges on clear and comprehensive communication channels across the entire organization, as well as through reporting mechanisms to the board and senior management. Detailed guidance is provided within this principle regarding risk communication strategies, information dissemination, reporting protocols, and the integration of risk systems to facilitate effective risk communication throughout the organization.

Principle 9: Compliance

This principle underscores the responsibility of the bank's board of directors in overseeing compliance risk management. The board is tasked with establishing a compliance function and approving policies and procedures for identifying, assessing, monitoring, reporting, and advising on compliance risk. An independent compliance function serves as a crucial element of the bank's second line of defense, ensuring adherence to applicable laws, regulations, and internal policies to maintain integrity in operations.

Principle 10: Internal audit

Principle 10 emphasizes the significance of the internal audit function in providing independent assurance to the board and supporting both board and senior management in fostering effective governance processes and ensuring the long-term stability of the bank. Serving as the third line of defense in the internal control system, the internal audit function should possess a clear mandate, be accountable to the board, and maintain independence from the activities it audits. Any removal of the chief audit executive from their position should be publicly disclosed, with reasons discussed with the bank's supervisor.

Principle 11: Compensation

This principle underscores the importance of the bank's remuneration structure in supporting sound corporate governance and risk management. The responsibility for overseeing management's implementation of the remuneration system for the entire bank lies with the board or, by its delegation, the compensation committee. This oversight includes reviewing outcomes related to the incentives created by the remuneration system.

Principle 12: Disclosure and transparency

Principle 12 emphasizes the importance of disclosure and transparency in the governance of the bank, ensuring that shareholders, depositors, other stakeholders, and market participants have access to adequate information. Banks should annually disclose their approach to board member selection, board composition, and the existence and frequency of board committees. Moreover, banks should apply the disclosure and transparency standards outlined in the OECD principles, providing key information about their risk exposures and management strategies while maintaining necessary confidentiality. Disclosure should be accurate, clear, and timely, especially for material, complex, or non-transparent activities, where information about purpose, strategies, structures, and related risks and controls should be provided.

Principle 13: The role of supervisors

Principle 13 underscores the crucial role of supervisors in guiding and overseeing corporate governance at banks. Supervisors are tasked with providing guidance and supervision, including through evaluations and regular interaction with boards and senior management. They should establish expectations for sound corporate governance, conduct thorough evaluations, and require banks to take corrective actions when necessary. Additionally, supervisors are expected to cooperate and share governance-related information with other relevant regulatory authorities.

It is worth mentioning that, similar to the OECD principles, these guidelines set forth by the Basel Committee are non-binding. They serve as a reference framework for policymakers, aiding in the development of legal and regulatory structures for governance that align with specific economic and social contexts. These principles are designed to evolve over time and offer flexibility to accommodate changing circumstances and emerging best practices in governance.

Additionally, the committee has defined governance in banks as "A set of relationships between a company's management, its board, its shareholders and other stakeholders which provides the structure through which the objectives of the company are set, and the means of attaining those objectives and monitoring performance.2 It helps define the way authority and responsibility are allocated and how corporate decisions are made." From this definition and the principles outlined earlier, it appears that there's a fundamental similarity in the essence and content of the desired governance system for both economic and financial organisations, particularly banks. Ultimately, such systems should prioritize protecting the interests of stakeholders by promoting prudent management practices and considering the diverse needs of all stakeholders within the organization, irrespective of their roles or affiliations.

3. Corporate Governance Mechanisms

There is a broad consensus among scholars that effectively incorporating the principles and values of corporate governance necessitates the utilization of a set of legal and regulatory processes. These processes and frameworks are often referred to in the literature as governance mechanisms, which can be categorized into two distinct types: internal and external mechanisms. This section will address the Internal Corporate Governance Mechanisms, while the following one will deal with the external mechanisms.

3.1. Internal corporate governance mechanisms

Internal corporate governance mechanisms refer to the policies, processes, and structures established by the organization and overseen by the board of directors to ensure effective governance and oversight of its management. These mechanisms are designed to align the interests of various stakeholders, promote accountability, and mitigate potential conflicts of interest as well as the asymmetry of information. Some key internal corporate governance mechanisms include: the board of directors, board committees, and ownership structure.

3.1.1 The board of directors

A board of directors is a deliberative assembly that represents the interests of a company's shareholders. This governing entity also provides guidance and advice to an organization's chief executive officer and executive leadership team. The board is responsible for general oversight of operations without directly involving themselves in day-to-day managerial tasks. Boards tend to adopt a more long-term strategic outlook, while the CEO and management team focus on immediate operational challenges. In recent years, corporate boards have placed increased emphasis on evaluating and mitigating the environmental and social impacts of the organization's activities.

To ensure the prosperous performance of the organization, the board of directors must address and execute several critical functions effectively.

The four primary tasks of the corporate governing body, as identified by the Institute of Directors (1999b), are:

- **Establish and maintain the organization's vision, mission, and values:** in order to effectively carry out this task, the board must:
  - Ascertain the company's overarching vision and mission to guide and set the trajectory for its current operations and future development.
  - Determine the core values to be promoted and embedded throughout the organization.
  - Establish and periodically review the organization's strategic goals.
  - Formulate and oversee the implementation of company-wide policies.
- **Establish Organizational Strategy and Structure**: this task involves the board undertaking the following actions:
  - Comprehensively review and assess present and future opportunities, threats, and risks present in the external environment, as well as the organization's current and prospective internal strengths, weaknesses, and risks.
  - Identify and evaluate strategic options, select those most suitable to pursue, and determine the appropriate means to support their implementation.
  - Establish the overarching business strategies and operational plans that underpin the organization's corporate-level strategy.
  - Ensure the company's organizational structure and institutional capabilities are optimally aligned to effectively execute the chosen strategies.
- **Delegate to, and Oversee, Management:** to properly address this task, the board should undertake the following actions:
  - Delegate appropriate authority to the executive management team and consistently monitor and evaluate their implementation of company policies, strategies, and operational plans.
  - Establish well-defined criteria to assess and track management's performance.
  - Ensure the organization maintains effective internal control systems.

- Facilitate clear and constructive communication channels with senior leadership.

- **Fulfill Accountability to Shareholders and Responsibility to Stakeholders**: this task requires the board to:
  - Ensure effective communication channels are maintained both for receiving input from and disseminating information to the company's shareholders and other relevant stakeholders.
  - Comprehend and duly consider the distinct interests of shareholders and pertinent stakeholder groups.
  - Systematically monitor relations with shareholders and stakeholders by proactively gathering and evaluating appropriate information.
  - Promote goodwill and garner support from shareholders and relevant stakeholders through active management of these critical relationships.

The members of a Corporation's Board of Directors can be systematically classified into the following distinct categories:

- **Internal Members (Executives)**

These are board directors who concurrently hold senior executive management positions within the organization. As both board members and organizational leaders, they provide direct operational oversight and strategic guidance, drawing upon their intimate knowledge of the company's inner workings. Internal board members are responsible for aligning the board's governance objectives with the executive team's day-to-day decision-making and implementation.

- **External (Independent) (Non-Executive) Members**

These are board directors who maintain complete independence from the company's executive management. As outsiders without any vested interest or direct affiliation, external/independent board members offer impartial perspectives and unbiased oversight. Their primary role is to advocate for the interests of the organization's shareholders and other key stakeholders, while providing objective counsel on the company's strategic direction and risk management. Independent directors are essential for ensuring robust corporate governance and accountability

- **Gray Members (External but Not Independent)**

These are board directors who, while not part of the executive management hierarchy, may have other professional, financial, or personal relationships that compromise their independence and objectivity. Gray members occupy a middle ground, as they are externally situated but do not meet the criteria for true independence. Examples include former executives, major shareholders, or relatives of company insiders. The presence of gray members on the board can potentially undermine the board's ability to provide unbiased oversight and represents a governance vulnerability that requires careful consideration.

Overall, it can be said that the Board of Directors is the primary governing body entrusted with advancing the diverse interests of the organization's stakeholders. In light of the inherent information asymmetry and potential conflicts of interest between executive management and the broader stakeholder community, the Board emerges as a crucial mechanism to monitor, direct, and hold the management team accountable for upholding stakeholder interests.

The Board's key responsibilities include appointing, overseeing, guiding, evaluating, and maintaining accountability for the executive leadership. Through these oversight functions, the Board aims to align the practices of management with the overarching objectives and concerns of the organization's stakeholders.

The principles of effective corporate governance emphasize the critical need for the Board of Directors to consistently act in a fair and impartial manner when balancing the varied interests of different stakeholder groups. This requires the Board to exercise independent judgment, maintain transparency, and demonstrate a commitment to ethical decision-making.

To effectively exercise its supervisory and oversight functions, the Board of Directors must possess certain key characteristics, the most critical of which are:

- **Independence**

The board must maintain a sufficient degree of independence from the executive management team in order to provide unbiased monitoring and objective guidance. This is a fundamental tenet of effective corporate governance, as it enables the board to exercise impartial oversight without undue influence or conflicts of interest.

Typically, this requires that a majority of the board members be independent, non-executive directors. These individuals must lack any personal, financial, or professional affiliations that could compromise their ability to make decisions solely in the best interests of the organization and its stakeholders.

Independent directors should have no material connection to the company beyond their board service. They should not be current or former employees, have significant business relationships with the firm, or have familial ties to executives. Their compensation should also be structured to avoid creating incentives that could sway their judgment.

The presence of a independent-majority board ensures that the supervisory and advisory functions of the directors are not unduly swayed by management's interests or biases. Independent members can provide an external perspective, challenge executive proposals, and hold management accountable without fear of repercussions. This arms-length relationship is essential for the board to execute its duties of oversight, strategic guidance, and conflict resolution in an objective manner.

- **Expertise and Diversity**

The board should collectively possess a robust breadth of relevant skills, knowledge, and experiences to enable comprehensive oversight of the organization's operations and strategic decision-making. This multifaceted expertise is essential for the board to effectively execute its governance responsibilities.

Board members should bring a diverse array of professional backgrounds and functional competencies to the table. This may involve directors with deep expertise in areas such as finance, accounting, risk management, industry-specific technical knowledge, human capital management, information technology, and corporate governance best practices.

The presence of directors with this caliber of specialized expertise allows the board to engage in substantive, nuanced discussions and make informed judgments on complex organizational matters. For example, directors with financial acumen can provide rigorous oversight of accounting practices and capital allocation decisions. Those with risk management backgrounds can help the board identify, assess, and mitigate strategic, operational, and compliance-related vulnerabilities. Industry veterans can offer invaluable insights into competitive dynamics, market trends, and technological disruptions.

Beyond just functional skills, the board should also reflect diversity in terms of personal backgrounds, cognitive approaches, and demographic characteristics. This multidimensional diversity enables the board to consider issues from a range of perspectives, challenge assumptions, and arrive at more well-rounded solutions. It also enhances the board's ability to understand and respond to the needs of the organization's diverse stakeholder groups.

- **The size**

The size of the board of directors is a critical determinant of its ability to function effectively and discharge its governance responsibilities. An optimal board size ensures a balanced composition, promotes active engagement, and fosters efficient decision-making processes.

An appropriately sized board strikes the right equilibrium between having a sufficient breadth of expertise and diverse perspectives while maintaining a manageable and cohesive group dynamic. Boards that are too small may lack the collective knowledge, skill sets, and resources required to provide comprehensive oversight across the organization's varied operations and risk areas. Conversely, excessively large boards can become unwieldy, hindering productive discussions, decision-making agility, and cohesion among directors.

Research and governance best practices generally recommend boards with 8-10 members, with many experts suggesting this range as an optimal target. This size facilitates active participation and engagement from all directors, enabling them to contribute meaningfully to discussions and deliberations. It also allows for the establishment of an effective committee structure, with adequate resources dedicated to specialized areas of oversight, such as audit, compensation, and governance.

- **Transparent Processes**

The board should maintain clear and transparent processes for decision-making, information sharing, and communication with stakeholders. This transparency is essential for upholding accountability and building trust with the organization's broader stakeholder community.

An appropriately sized board can contribute to more effective governance by promoting robust discussions, efficient decision-making, and a balanced distribution of oversight responsibilities. When the board size is well-calibrated, directors can engage in candid dialogue, challenge assumptions, and leverage their collective expertise to navigate complex issues and drive informed decision-making. This, in turn, enhances the board's ability to provide strategic guidance, exercise independent oversight, and contribute to the long-term success and value creation of the organization.

Transparent decision-making requires the board to document its processes for evaluating issues, deliberating on options, and arriving at final determinations. This includes detailing the information sources consulted, the analytical frameworks applied, and the rationale underlying key decisions. Making these decision-making protocols visible enhances the credibility of the board's actions and allows for external scrutiny.

Similarly, the board must ensure transparent information sharing, both within the organization and with relevant stakeholders. This involves establishing well-defined channels and cadences for the dissemination of pertinent financial, operational, and strategic data. Proactive, consistent communication enables stakeholders to remain informed and engaged, rather than relying on speculative or incomplete information.

Transparent communication with stakeholders is also crucial. The board should maintain open dialogues with shareholders, regulators, customers, employees, and other key parties. This ongoing engagement allows the board to better understand and address the concerns of diverse stakeholder groups. It also strengthens the board's accountability, as stakeholders can provide direct feedback and exercise oversight of the board's activities.

Upholding these principles of transparency helps to build trust in the board's oversight and fosters a culture of integrity within the organization. When stakeholders can clearly see the board's decision-making processes and access relevant information, it enhances perceptions of fairness, ethical conduct, and responsible governance.

The board should codify its transparency commitments through formal policies and procedures. Regular audits of the organization's disclosure practices and stakeholder communication channels can also help the board identify areas for improvement in its transparency efforts.

- **Continuous Improvement**

The board should regularly assess its own performance and proactively seek opportunities to enhance its overall effectiveness. This commitment to ongoing enhancement is essential for ensuring the board can adapt to evolving organizational needs and industry best practices.

Regular self-assessment is a critical component of the board's continuous improvement process. This involves systematically evaluating the board's execution of its core oversight, advisory, and accountability responsibilities. Metrics such as meeting attendance, quality of discussions, decision-making processes, and responsiveness to stakeholder concerns can all provide valuable insights into the board's strengths and areas for development.

Based on these self-assessments, the board should then identify targeted training and educational programs to strengthen the collective knowledge and skills of its members. This may include workshops on emerging industry trends, changing regulatory environments, advances in corporate governance standards, or techniques for effective board leadership and collaboration.

The recruitment of new board members also presents an opportunity to enhance the board's capabilities. The nominating committee should actively seek out candidates who can fill any gaps in the board's expertise, diversity, or independent oversight. Onboarding programs that provide comprehensive orientation for new directors are essential for rapidly integrating them into the board's operations.

Additionally, the board should routinely benchmark its practices against recognized governance frameworks and industry peers. This environmental scanning allows the board to identify opportunities to implement more effective policies, processes and structures. Examples may include enhancing board committee structures, improving information flows, or adopting leading approaches to director compensation and performance management.

By embracing a mindset of continuous improvement, the board can ensure it maintains the agility, expertise, and independence necessary to fulfill its critical oversight role on behalf of the organization and its stakeholders. This ongoing enhancement is a hallmark of boards that exhibit excellence in corporate governance.

- **Effective Committee Structure**

The board should establish a well-designed system of specialized committees to allow for deeper examination of key focus areas and a more efficient division of oversight responsibilities. The use of board committees is a hallmark of robust corporate governance, as it enables the directors to leverage their collective expertise and allocate their time and attention more strategically.

The following section will provide an overview of the Common essential board committees.

3.1.2. Board Committees

- **Audit Committee**

The audit committee holds the critical responsibility of overseeing the organization's financial reporting processes, internal control systems, and risk management practices. This committee serves as a vital safeguard, ensuring the integrity and reliability of the company's financial information and operational controls.

The audit committee's primary duties include:

- **Financial Reporting Oversight:** The committee closely monitors the organization's accounting policies, financial disclosures, and reporting procedures. This involves reviewing quarterly and annual financial statements, as well as discussing any significant accounting judgments, estimates, or unusual transactions with management and the independent auditors.
- **Internal Control Systems:** The committee evaluates the design and operating effectiveness of the company's internal control framework. This includes assessing the policies, processes, and technologies used to ensure the accuracy of financial records, protect assets, and promote compliance with laws and regulations.
- **Risk Management Supervision:** The committee provides oversight of the organization's enterprise risk management practices. It reviews the company's risk profile, evaluates the adequacy of risk mitigation strategies, and ensures appropriate processes are in place to identify, assess, and address emerging risks.

To effectively execute its critical oversight responsibilities, the audit committee must be characterized by:

- **Independence**

The audit committee must maintain a high degree of independence from the company's executive management in order to provide objective, unbiased oversight. This typically requires that the committee be composed entirely of non-executive, independent directors who lack any personal, financial, or professional affiliations that could compromise their impartiality.

Independent audit committee members are able to challenge management decisions, raise difficult questions, and escalate concerns without fear of retaliation or undue influence. Their arms-length relationship with the executive team enables them to serve as a crucial check on management's financial reporting practices, internal control systems, and risk management approaches.

The company's governing documents, as well as relevant regulatory guidelines, often mandate specific requirements around audit committee independence. Regular assessments of member independence and the committee's overall autonomy are critical to upholding this essential principle of sound corporate governance.

- **Expertise**

In addition to independence, the audit committee must also collectively possess a high degree of financial expertise and accounting acumen to effectively execute its oversight responsibilities. Committee members should have the necessary skills to understand complex accounting standards, interpret financial statements, and evaluate the appropriateness of the company's financial reporting and control mechanisms.

Relevant expertise may include backgrounds in areas such as corporate finance, public accounting, financial risk management, and data analytics. Committee members with professional certifications, such as Certified Public Accountants (CPAs) or Chartered Financial Analysts (CFAs), can further enhance the committee's technical competence.

The presence of financially literate, technically proficient audit committee members enables the group to engage in substantive, insightful discussions with management and the independent auditors. This expertise allows the committee to identify potential issues, offer constructive guidance, and arrive at well-informed judgments that serve to protect the company's financial integrity and safeguard stakeholder interests.

- **Compensation Committee**

The Compensation Committee plays a crucial role in aligning executive compensation with the company's strategic objectives and long-term value creation. Its primary responsibilities include:

- **Establishing Executive Compensation Philosophy and Policies**
  - Developing a comprehensive compensation philosophy that attracts, retains, and motivates top executive talent.
  - Determining the appropriate mix of salary, short-term incentives, long-term incentives, and other benefits.
  - Ensuring compensation policies are competitive, fair, and aligned with market practices and industry peers.
- **Setting Executive Compensation Levels**
  - Evaluating and approving compensation packages for the CEO and other senior executives.
  - Reviewing and approving performance goals and metrics tied to incentive compensation plans.

- Considering factors such as individual performance, company performance, and shareholder returns.

- **Linking Pay to Performance**
  - Designing incentive plans that reward executives for achieving specific financial, operational, and strategic objectives.
  - Ensuring a strong correlation between executive compensation and the company's overall performance and shareholder value creation.
  - Evaluating the appropriateness of incentive plan payouts based on performance outcomes.
- **Managing Talent and Succession Planning**
  - Overseeing executive development and leadership succession plans.
  - Assessing the strength of the company's leadership pipeline and talent management strategies.
  - Ensuring effective succession planning for key executive roles.
- **Oversight and Disclosure**
  - Reviewing and approving the Compensation Discussion and Analysis (CD&A) section of the company's proxy statement.
  - Ensuring compliance with relevant regulations and disclosure requirements related to executive compensation.
  - Engaging with shareholders and proxy advisory firms on compensation-related matters.

The Compensation Committee typically includes directors with expertise in areas such as human capital management, organizational design, executive compensation practices, and risk management. Their collective knowledge and experience enable them to navigate the complex challenges of attracting and retaining top talent while ensuring pay practices are aligned with shareholder interests and corporate objectives.

- **Nominating/Governance Committee**

The Nominating/Governance Committee plays a crucial role in safeguarding the integrity and effectiveness of the board's governance framework. Its primary responsibilities revolve around three key areas:

- **Board Composition and Nomination Process**
  - Establishing criteria for board membership, considering factors such as skills, experience, diversity, and independence standards.
  - Conducting comprehensive searches and evaluations to identify qualified director candidates.
  - Recommending nominees to the full board for election or re-election at the annual shareholders' meeting.
  - Overseeing the board's refreshment process, including director tenure, retirement, and succession planning.
- **Board Evaluation and Performance Assessment**
  - Developing and implementing a robust process for evaluating the performance of the board, its committees, and individual directors.
  - Facilitating self-assessments and peer evaluations to identify strengths, weaknesses, and areas for improvement.
  - Analyzing the board's overall composition, dynamics, and culture to ensure optimal effectiveness.
  - Recommending actions to enhance board performance, such as restructuring committees or providing additional training and development opportunities.
- **Corporate Governance Framework and Best Practices**
  - Developing and periodically reviewing the company's corporate governance guidelines and policies.
  - Monitoring emerging trends, regulatory changes, and stakeholder expectations related to governance practices.
  - Ensuring the company's governance framework aligns with industry best practices and legal requirements.
  - Overseeing the implementation and adherence to governance policies and procedures across the organization.

- Facilitating constructive dialogue with shareholders on governance-related matters and considering their perspectives

3.1.3. Ownership structure

Ownership structure refers to the distribution of equity ownership among different types of shareholders, such as individual investors, institutional investors, founding families, or other corporate entities. The nature and concentration of ownership can significantly influence the dynamics of corporate governance and the alignment of interests between shareholders and management. Two main types of ownership structures are concentrated ownership and dispersed ownership, each with distinct implications for corporate governance.

- **Concentrated Ownership**

Concentrated ownership exists when a significant portion of a company's shares is held by a small number of individuals, families, or institutional investors. This ownership structure has several implications for corporate governance:

- **Stronger monitoring and control:** Large shareholders with significant stakes have a vested interest in the company's performance and are more likely to actively monitor management's actions, demand accountability, and exert influence over strategic decisions.
- **Potential for shareholder activism:** Concentrated owners may engage in shareholder activism, using their voting power and influence to push for changes in corporate policies, board composition, or management practices when they are dissatisfied with the company's direction or performance.

- **Board representation:** Major shareholders often have representation on the board of directors, allowing them to directly participate in governance processes and decision-making.
- **Alignment of interests:** Concentrated ownership can lead to better alignment between shareholders' and management's interests, as both parties have a significant stake in the company's long-term success.
- **Potential for conflicts of interest:** However, concentrated ownership can also give rise to conflicts of interest, particularly if the controlling shareholders prioritize their personal interests over those of minority shareholders.

- **Dispersed Ownership**

Dispersed ownership refers to a situation where a company's shares are widely held by numerous individual investors, with no single entity holding a controlling stake. This ownership structure has different implications for corporate governance:

- **Separation of ownership and control:** With no dominant shareholder, there is a greater separation between ownership (shareholders) and control (management), potentially leading to agency problems and misalignment of interests.
- **Reliance on external governance mechanisms:** Companies with dispersed ownership tend to rely more heavily on external governance mechanisms, such as independent boards, regulatory oversight, and market forces (e.g., takeover threats) to monitor and discipline management.
- **Shareholder activism challenges:** It is more difficult for individual shareholders to exert significant influence or engage in activism due to the collective action problem and the relatively small stakes held by each investor.

- **Importance of board independence:** The board of directors plays a critical role in representing the interests of dispersed shareholders and ensuring effective oversight of management.
- **Emphasis on transparency and disclosure:** Robust disclosure and transparency practices become increasingly important to enable dispersed shareholders to make informed decisions and hold management accountable.

Both concentrated and dispersed ownership structures have their advantages and potential drawbacks in terms of corporate governance. Understanding a company's specific ownership structure is crucial for assessing the dynamics of power, accountability, and decision-making within the organization.

3.2. External Corporate Governance Mechanisms

These refer to the monitoring and disciplining forces that exist outside the firm's internal controls. The company lacks direct jurisdiction over these external mechanisms. They primarily manifest through the power and influence that various stakeholders can exert upon the organization. The significance of external corporate governance mechanisms lies in their ability to promote sound managerial practices and accountability within the firm.

3.2.2. External audit

An external audit is an independent review of a company's annual financial statements and reports conducted by an external auditor. The objective is to provide an impartial professional opinion on whether the financial information accurately represents the company's financial position in accordance with accounting standards. External audits aim to ensure the reliability and credibility of the accounting information disclosed by the company.

External audits are a prominent mechanism stakeholders rely on to verify management's accounting practices and disclosures. The external auditor plays an important role in enhancing the reliability and credibility of financial information within the agency relationship between management and stakeholders. The effectiveness of external audits depends largely on the auditor's independence, adherence to standards, ethics, and quality control. Independence is the most crucial factor, requiring no material interests with the client that could impair objectivity.

Independence is achieved when the auditor has no direct/indirect interests that could influence their behavior. It involves not being a shareholder with control, former employee, having family ties with executives, acting as an advisor, being a major supplier/customer, or contractor. Periodic auditor rotation, such as every 3 years as per regulations like Sarbanes-Oxley, helps maintain independence.

In essence, external audits serve as an independent monitoring mechanism in corporate governance by providing assurance over financial reporting. However, their effectiveness hinges critically on the auditor's ability to remain truly independent and objective.

Independence is achieved when the auditor has no direct or indirect interests that could influence their behavior or objectivity. This requires the auditor to be free from any conflicts of interest or undue influences that could compromise their ability to remain impartial and objective during the audit process. There are several factors that can impair an auditor's independence:

- **Financial interests:** The auditor should not hold any direct financial interests, such as being a shareholder with controlling power or the ability to influence the management of the audited company directly. This could create conflicts and pressure to issue a favorable opinion.
- **Employment relationships:** The auditor should not be a current employee of the company being audited or have been employed by the company in an executive/decision-making capacity within the past few years (e.g., 3 years). Such relationships could bias the auditor's judgement.

- **Family and personal relationships:** Auditors should not have close family members employed as executives or decision-makers within the audited company, as this personal association could impact their objectivity.
- **Non-audit services:** Providing significant non-audit services (e.g. consulting, bookkeeping) to an audit client could create a mutuality of interests that threatens independence.
- **Financial dependencies:** If a substantial portion of the audit firm's revenue comes from one client, economic pressures could impair independence.

To mitigate these threats, regulations like the Sarbanes-Oxley Act have implemented requirements such as mandatory audit partner rotation every 5 years and prohibiting auditors from providing certain non-audit services. This helps prevent familiarity threats and conflicts of interest from developing over time.

Additionally, maintaining a robust system of quality controls within the audit firm is essential for ensuring audits are performed with due professional care and objectivity. This involves implementing comprehensive policies and procedures that address key areas such as:

- Client acceptance and continuance procedures to evaluate potential independence threats.
- Engagement performance including supervision, staff training, and application of auditing standards.
- Consultation processes for resolving complex accounting/auditing issues.
- Internal inspection programs to monitor compliance with policies and professional standards.

Adhering to professional ethics standards established by governing bodies (e.g. AICPA, IFAC) is paramount. Key ethics principles auditors must uphold include integrity, objectivity, professional competence, confidentiality, and professional behavior. Having a robust ethics infrastructure with training, counseling hotlines and disciplinary mechanisms reinforces ethical conduct.

Nurturing an independent culture and mindset within the audit firm is crucial for objectivity. This is fostered through firm leadership emphasizing auditor independence as a core value and not tolerating actions that undermine it. Measures like:

- Accountability and compensation systems rewarding independent judgement, not revenue generation.
- Robust policies prohibiting financial interests, business relationships or gifts impairing independence.
- Continuing professional education stressing public interest responsibilities and skepticism.
- Open communication channels for staff to report potential independence violations.

By institutionalizing these measures, audit firms can create an environment where auditors internalize an independent mindset - maintaining objectivity, integrity and professional skepticism on each engagement. This commitment to quality, ethics and independence is vital for auditors to fulfill their public watchdog role effectively and retain stakeholder trust.

3.2.3. Legal/regulatory system and environment

The legal/regulatory system refers to the laws, regulations, and enforcement mechanisms that govern corporate behavior and practices. It establishes the "rules of the game" that companies must operate within. Laws and regulations set minimum standards for corporate governance practices, financial reporting, auditing, and disclosure requirements that companies must adhere to. Regulatory bodies like the Securities and Exchange Commission (SEC) have enforcement powers to investigate violations and impose penalties on companies and individuals for non-compliance. Legal provisions allow shareholders to pursue class-action lawsuits against companies for corporate misconduct, fraud, or misrepresentation. Regulations often mandate certain governance structures like independent boards, audit committees, and internal control certifications. Disclosure rules require companies to publicly report information, increasing transparency for investors and the market.

The legal/regulatory environment acts as an external disciplining force on companies and management through the threat of legal/regulatory sanctions and investor lawsuits. Common governance standards create a level playing field and comparability across firms. Regulations aim to protect shareholder rights and ensure management accountability. A strong, well-enforced legal system promotes investor confidence in capital markets.

The comprehensiveness and quality of laws/regulations is crucial. The legal framework needs to address all key aspects of corporate governance - board responsibilities, executive compensation, related party transactions, disclosure requirements, shareholder rights etc. Principles-based regulations provide flexibility, while excessive reliance on rigid rules can lead to a compliance-based mindset. Well-designed regulations aligned with best practices enhance their effectiveness.

The independence and resourcing of regulatory bodies like the SEC is vital for robust oversight and enforcement. Well-funded agencies with technical expertise, investigative powers and independence from political/corporate influence can act as credible deterrents against misconduct. Frequent leadership changes or resource constraints can undermine regulatory effectiveness.

Consistent interpretation and enforcement of rules across companies and over time is important. Inconsistent application due to ambiguities, loopholes or discretionary enforcement can create an uneven playing field. Clear guidance, common legal precedents set through judicial decisions, and data-driven, risk-based enforcement help uphold rule of law.

The private litigation environment, especially securities class-action lawsuits, impacts corporate behavior. The threat of hefty damages awards incentivizes companies to maintain robust governance. However, a litigation environment prone to frivolous lawsuits can impose cumbersome compliance costs.

For multinational companies, the extraterritorial reach and coordination between home and host country regulations is relevant. Cross-listing requirements, differing governance codes and accounting standards need to be navigated. Regulatory convergence and mutual recognition agreements can enhance a consistent governance framework globally.

Other factors like the general respect for rule of law, control of corruption and political stability in a country also influence how effectively regulations can be implemented in practice. A holistic legal infrastructure promoting ethical business conduct is necessary.

In essence, when laws/regulations are comprehensive, enforced consistently by well-resourced independent agencies, buttressed by private liabilities and extraterritorial coordination - the legal environment becomes a robust external governance mechanism.

3.2.4. Financial markets

Financial markets refer to the stock markets, debt markets, and other capital markets where a company's securities are traded. The trading of a firm's shares and bonds subjects it to market scrutiny and discipline. The market for corporate control - the threat of hostile takeovers and proxy contests - serves to discipline underperforming management teams. Poor governance can depress the stock price, increasing the cost of capital and making it more difficult to raise funds. It is also associated with higher borrowing costs, lower debt ratings, and difficulties accessing debt markets. Analysts evaluate corporate governance as part of their research, influencing investor perceptions and confidence. Investors can short sell shares if they perceive overvaluation or governance risks, putting downward price pressure.

Financial markets provide several mechanisms for governance. Stock and debt price movements send important feedback signals to managers about governance perceptions. The market for corporate control incentivizes managers to maximize firm value to avoid hostile takeovers. Markets provide independent, low-cost monitoring compared to direct shareholder oversight. Analysts, ratings agencies auditors produce and assess governance-related information for the market. Wher corporate governance concerns are efficiently priced by financial markets, it exert external pressures on companies to adopt sound practices or face valuatior discounts and higher capital costs.

Developed, liquid capital markets with sufficient trading activity are necessary fo the market forces to function properly. Thin trading or illiquid markets can lead t stale prices that do not accurately reflect a company's governance quality. A critica mass of investors and analysts covering the stock is required. More develope markets also tend to have higher institutional ownership which strengthen governance.

Protection of shareholder rights, especially for minority investors, is vital. Market cannot exert disciplining pressure if shareholders lack the ability to vote, cal meetings, inspect records, or pursue control transactions like proxy fights. Robus shareholder rights enable investors to take actions to improve governance.

Transparent and reliable disclosure of financial, governance and operationa information is critical for market participants to assess companies properly. Lack c disclosures or doubts about data integrity hamper the markets' informatior processing ability. Requirements for comprehensive, audited and timely reportin enhance pricing efficiency.

The incentives and accountability of brokers, analysts and rating agencies must b aligned with investor interests rather than corporate issuers. Conflicts lik investment banking ties or selective disclosures can compromise governanc assessments. Regulations addressing these conflicts strengthen sell-side credibility

Institutional investors like mutual funds, pension funds and activist hedge fund play a major role in governance through markets. Their large ownership stakes engaged monitoring and willingness to intervene through voting or publicit campaigns amplify market discipline. Markets with fragmented retail ownership ar less effective governance mechanisms.

Sophisticated traders like arbitrageurs also contribute by rapidly incorporating governance information into prices through trading strategies like risk arbitrage during takeovers. Their information processing expertise enhances pricing efficiency related to governance factors.

Finally, a strong legal environment, credible regulatory oversight and robust investor protection rules underpin the proper functioning of markets as an external governance force.

3.2.5. Rating agencies

Rating agencies are independent organizations that assess and rate the creditworthiness and risk profiles of companies and their debt securities. Major agencies include Moody's, S&P, Fitch, etc. Agencies evaluate a company's corporate governance as part of their credit risk analysis for determining credit ratings. Some agencies provide separate corporate governance ratings/scores in addition to credit ratings. Published ratings act as a signal to debt and equity markets about governance quality. Lower ratings can increase a company's borrowing costs and difficulty accessing capital markets.

In their governance assessments, rating agencies look at factors such as board independence, oversight and quality, management credibility and risk appetite, shareholder rights and treatment of minority investors, financial reporting transparency and disclosures, as well as risk management systems and internal controls. Rating agencies act as an independent source of monitoring and opinion on governance practices. Poor governance ratings can negatively impact a firm's access to capital and cost of funds. Agencies also establish evaluation criteria that set benchmarks for governance best practices.

The reputational incentives and desire to maintain credibility act as a key driver for rating agencies to be accurate and independent in their assessments. Their long-term business model relies on investors trusting their opinions. Any perception of bias or inaccuracy can severely damage their brand equity built over decades. This reputational capital provides incentives for rigorous and objective analysis.

Robust rating methodologies that comprehensively and meaningfully incorporate governance factors into the assessment process are necessary. Ratings models that neglect or pay lip service to governance risk threaten to undermine their effectiveness. A systematic framework considering key areas like board structures, executive compensation policies, related party transactions, risk oversight etc. enhances rating quality.

The issuer-paid model, where agencies are compensated by the companies they rate, represents a potential conflict of interest that must be carefully managed. Economic incentives to appease issuers could consciously or unconsciously influence ratings. Stringent internal controls, prohibitions on consulting, and rotating analysis teams are required to mitigate this risk.

Independent regulatory oversight by bodies like the Securities and Exchange Commission can further reinforce the agencies' governance role. Monitoring and scrutiny over methodologies, managing conflicts of interest, and requiring transparency enhances accountability. Holding rating agencies legally liable for gross negligence through investor lawsuits also strengthens their due diligence incentives.

When rating agencies act as truly independent arbiters, free from conflicts and with high-quality governance assessment processes, their published ratings serve as a very visible external signal to debt and equity investors about a company's governance quality. This market scrutiny allows investors to efficiently price governance risks into valuations and demand higher returns from poorly-governed firms as compensation, exerting discipline.

However, if conflicts fester, rating processes lack rigor, or regulatory oversight is lax, the governance role of ratings can be compromised. Recent controversies like inflated mortgage security ratings preceding the 2008 financial crisis highlight the potential governance failures when misaligned incentives exist in the ratings industry.

CHAPTER 4
COMPARATIVE ANALYSIS OF CORPORATE GOVERNANCE MODELS ADOPTED IN THE WORLD

Chapter 4: Comparative Analysis of Corporate Governance Models Adopted in the World

In this chapter, we undertake a comparative a comparative analysis of corporate governance systems prevalent worldwide. We focus on two primary models: the Anglo-Saxon model and the continental European model, often referred to as the German-Japanese model. Furthermore, we offer insights into the corporate governance landscape in Algeria.

1. The Anglo-Saxon model

The Anglo-Saxon model of corporate governance is primarily found in countries like the United States, United Kingdom, Canada, and Australia. It stands as a prominent example of a shareholder-centric approach to corporate governance. The core principle of this model revolves around maximizing shareholder value, treating shareholders as the ultimate owners of the company and prioritizing their interest above those of other stakeholders.

This model operates within a system of dispersed ownership, where shares are widely held by individual and institutional investors, leading to a separation of ownership and control. Companies typically adopt a one-tier board structure consisting of both executive and non-executive directors. Executive directors are involved in the day-to-day operations of the company, while non-executive directors, often with significant expertise and independence, provide objective oversight and strategic guidance. The board plays a crucial role in ensuring management accountability and aligning company actions with shareholder interests.

Market forces and shareholder activism serve as key mechanisms to discipline management in the Anglo-Saxon model. The threat of hostile takeovers, shareholder resolutions, and the influence of proxy advisory firms incentivize management to prioritize shareholder returns and act in their best interests. Transparency and disclosure are crucial aspects, with companies obligated to provide regular financial reports and other relevant information to ensure informed shareholder decision-making.

Regulation in this model tends to be principles-based rather than rules-based, offering broad guidelines and relying on market forces and self-regulation to ensure good corporate governance. However, regulations like the Sarbanes-Oxley Act in the US demonstrate a move towards more prescriptive rules following major corporate scandals.

1.1. Strengths of the Anglo-Saxon model

- **Efficiency and Innovation**

The Anglo-Saxon model's focus on maximizing shareholder value creates strong incentives for management to allocate the company's resources in the most efficient manner possible. This efficiency-driven approach encourages companies to continuously innovate and take calculated risks in order to generate higher returns for shareholders.

The pressure to demonstrate superior financial performance and shareholder returns spurs companies to adopt new technologies, develop innovative products and services, and explore novel business strategies. This dynamic environment can foster an entrepreneurial spirit and drive companies to push the boundaries of what is possible within their industries.

- **Shareholder Protection**

The Anglo-Saxon model places a strong emphasis on shareholder rights and active engagement, which helps to ensure greater accountability of management to the company's owners.

Robust transparency requirements compel companies to regularly disclose financial information, operational details, and other key data to shareholders, enabling them to make informed decisions.

Shareholders are empowered to voice their concerns and influence company decisions through mechanisms such as proxy voting, shareholder resolutions, and the threat of potential hostile takeovers.

This focus on shareholder protection helps to align the interests of management with those of the owners, reducing the risk of managerial opportunism or self-serving behavior.

- **Attracting Capital**

The Anglo-Saxon model's emphasis on shareholder returns and transparent reporting standards can make companies operating within this framework attractive to both domestic and international investors.

The promise of consistent dividend payouts and potential for capital appreciation through stock price growth appeals to a wide range of investors, from individual retail shareholders to large institutional funds. By successfully attracting investment capital, companies can finance growth initiatives, fund research and development, and expand their operations, ultimately contributing to economic development and job creation.

The availability of abundant and relatively low-cost capital in this model can provide companies with a strategic advantage in competitive markets.

1.2. Weaknesses of the Anglo-Saxon model

- **Short-Termism**

The intense pressure on companies to deliver consistent and immediate returns to shareholders can create a strong incentive for management to focus on short-term profit maximization rather than long-term value creation.

This short-term orientation can lead to underinvestment in critical areas such as research and development, employee training, and infrastructure improvements that are essential for sustained competitiveness and growth.

In an effort to meet quarterly earnings targets and appease impatient shareholders, companies may forgo important strategic initiatives or cut costs in ways that compromise the long-term health and resilience of the business.

The short-term mindset can also discourage companies from investing in projects with uncertain but potentially transformative payoffs, as the immediate impact on shareholder returns may be negative.

This myopic focus on the near-term can ultimately undermine a company's ability to adapt to changing market conditions and technological disruptions, jeopardizing its long-term viability.

- **Social Inequality**

The Anglo-Saxon model's singular focus on maximizing shareholder wealth can exacerbate income inequality by channeling a disproportionate share of corporate profits to a small group of investors, rather than distributing the gains more broadly among various stakeholders.

By prioritizing shareholder interests over the needs of other stakeholders, such as employees, local communities, and the environment, the model can lead to the concentration of wealth in the hands of a few, while neglecting the wellbeing of the wider population.

This can contribute to social tensions, erosion of public trust in corporations, and a growing sense of economic disenfranchisement among marginalized groups.

The widening wealth gap and social inequalities stemming from the Anglo-Saxon model's shareholder-centric approach can have detrimental effects on social cohesion, political stability, and long-term economic prosperity.

- **Agency Problems**

The separation of ownership and control inherent in the Anglo-Saxon model can create agency problems, where professional managers (agents) may pursue their own interests at the expense of the shareholders (principals).

Executives, driven by personal incentives such as compensation packages and career advancement, may make decisions that prioritize their own interests over those of the company's owners.

This misalignment of interests can manifest in excessive risk-taking, empire building, short-term opportunism, and other forms of managerial behavior that are detrimental to shareholder value.

The dispersed ownership structure and the relative lack of direct oversight by shareholders can exacerbate these agency problems, making it more challenging for owners to effectively monitor and discipline management.

Addressing agency problems in the Anglo-Saxon model often requires strengthening corporate governance mechanisms, such as independent boards, robust performance-based compensation structures, and shareholder activism.

1.3. Evolution and Adaptation

Despite the criticisms leveled against the Anglo-Saxon model of corporate governance, it continues to evolve and adapt to changing societal and market demands. There are several notable trends and developments that are shaping the ongoing transformation of this model.

- **Embracing Environmental, Social, and Governance (ESG) Factors**

There is a growing recognition among companies operating within the Anglo-Saxon framework of the importance of environmental, social, and governance (ESG) considerations in their decision-making and strategy.
Many companies are proactively adopting sustainability initiatives, such as reducing carbon emissions, improving resource efficiency, and enhancing workplace diversity and inclusion.
By incorporating ESG factors into their business operations and reporting, companies are demonstrating a broader commitment to stakeholder interests, beyond just maximizing shareholder value.
This shift towards more holistic corporate responsibility is being driven by a combination of stakeholder demands, regulatory changes, and the realization that long-term business success is closely tied to environmental and social stewardship.

- **Engaging with a Broader Range of Stakeholders**

Traditionally, the Anglo-Saxon model has been primarily focused on serving the interests of shareholders. However, there is an increasing acknowledgment that the long-term viability of companies depends on addressing the concerns of a wider range of stakeholders.
Companies are now engaging more actively with employees, local communities, suppliers, and other affected parties to understand their needs and incorporate their perspectives into corporate decision-making.
This stakeholder-inclusive approach recognizes that the success of a business is intertwined with the well-being of the various groups and communities it interacts with and relies upon.
By fostering stronger relationships and aligning interests with a broader range of stakeholders, companies can enhance their social license to operate and build more sustainable business models.

- **Mitigating Short-Termism through Institutional Investors**

The rise of institutional investors, such as pension funds, sovereign wealth funds and asset management firms, with longer-term investment horizons is helping to mitigate the issue of short-termism in the Anglo-Saxon model.

These large institutional investors, with their significant holdings and influence, are increasingly advocating for companies to focus on long-term value creation, rather than solely pursuing short-term profit maximization.

By engaging with company management, exercising their voting rights, and promoting sustainable business practices, institutional investors are helping to shift the balance away from the excessive focus on quarterly results and towards a more strategic, long-term perspective.

This trend is being further amplified by the growing importance of ESG considerations in the investment decision-making process of these institutional investors.

2. The Continental Europe & Japan Model

In contrast to the Anglo-Saxon approach, the corporate governance model prevalent in Continental Europe and Japan is often characterized as a stakeholder-centric system. This model emphasizes the interests of a broader range of stakeholders including employees, creditors, suppliers, and the local community, rather than solely focusing on maximizing shareholder value.

The ownership structure in this model is typically more concentrated, with large institutional investors, such as banks, insurance companies, and industrial conglomerates, holding significant stakes in companies. This concentrated ownership structure allows for more active monitoring and engagement by major shareholders, who often have long-term investment horizons and close ties with the companies they invest in.

Companies in this model typically adopt a two-tier board structure, consisting of a management board (Vorstand in Germany, directoire in France) and a supervisory board (Aufsichtsrat in Germany, conseil de surveillance in France). The management board is responsible for the day-to-day operations and strategic decision-making, while the supervisory board oversees and advises the management team, often with representatives from various stakeholder groups. Employee representation on the supervisory board, known as "co-determination," is a key feature of this model in countries like Germany and the Netherlands.

Stakeholders, such as employees, creditors, and local communities, play a more prominent role in the decision-making process and have a stronger voice in corporate affairs. Labor unions and works councils often have a significant influence on corporate policies, particularly those related to employment, working conditions, and social welfare. Companies are expected to consider the impact of their decisions on various stakeholder groups, rather than solely focusing on shareholder interests.

The Continental Europe & Japan Model is characterized by a stronger reliance on bank financing and long-term relationships with lenders, rather than a heavy emphasis on public equity markets and shareholder-driven capital allocation. The capital markets in these countries are often less developed and less liquid compared to those in the Anglo-Saxon model, with a lower degree of dispersed ownership and shareholder activism.

The regulatory framework in this model tends to be more rules-based, with detailed laws and regulations governing corporate governance practices, employee rights, and stakeholder engagement. There is a greater emphasis on compliance with specific rules and guidelines, rather than a principles-based, market-driven approach to corporate governance.

2.1. Strengths of the Continental Europe & Japan Model

- **Stakeholder Consideration**

The stakeholder-centric approach of the Continental Europe & Japan Model ensures that the interests of a broader range of stakeholders, beyond just shareholders, are taken into account in corporate decision-making.

This inclusive approach can lead to more sustainable and socially responsible business practices, as companies strive to balance the needs and concerns of employees, suppliers, creditors, and local communities.

By considering the impact of their actions on various stakeholder groups, companies can foster stronger relationships and build a more reliable ecosystem for their operations.

- **Long-Term Orientation**

The concentrated ownership structure and the reliance on bank financing in this model encourage a longer-term perspective on value creation.

Companies are less burdened by the pressures of short-term shareholder demands and can instead focus on long-term investments in research, development, and employee training.

This long-term focus can enhance the competitiveness and resilience of companies as they are better positioned to weather economic downturns and adapt to changing market conditions.

- **Stability and Consensus-Building**

The two-tier board structure and the active involvement of stakeholders in the decision-making process promote stability and consensus-building within the organization.

The presence of employee representatives on the supervisory board, for example can help to align the interests of the workforce with those of the company, reducing the potential for conflicts and labor unrest.

This consensus-driven approach can foster a more collaborative and harmonious corporate culture, which can be beneficial for the company's overall performance and reputation.

2.2. Weaknesses of the Continental Europe & Japan Model

- **Potential Rigidity**

The more rules-based regulatory environment and the strong influence of certain stakeholder groups in the Continental Europe & Japan Model can lead to a less flexible and adaptable system.

The detailed laws and regulations governing corporate governance practices, as well as the active involvement of labor unions and other stakeholders in decision-making, can create bureaucratic hurdles and slow down the decision-making process.

This rigidity may hinder a company's ability to quickly respond to changing market conditions, technological disruptions, or emerging competitive challenges, potentially compromising its ability to innovate and maintain a competitive edge.

- **Potential for Inefficiency**

The multiple layers of oversight and the need to balance the interests of various stakeholders in this model can sometimes result in slower decision-making and a less efficient allocation of resources.

The two-tier board structure, with the management board and the supervisory board, can introduce an additional level of bureaucracy and coordination challenges, which may slow down the execution of strategic initiatives.

The requirement to consider the concerns of a broad range of stakeholders, while important for social responsibility, can also lead to compromises and trade-offs that may not always optimize for shareholder value or overall economic efficiency.

- **Challenges in Attracting Capital**

The concentrated ownership structure and the lower level of shareholder influence in the Continental Europe & Japan Model may make these markets less attractive to some international investors, particularly those who prioritize shareholder rights and liquidity.

The relative lack of dispersed ownership and active shareholder engagement compared to the Anglo-Saxon model, can be perceived as a barrier to transparency and investor protection, potentially limiting access to capital from global financial markets.

Companies in this model may face higher costs of capital or struggle to secure funding for ambitious growth plans, as investors may be deterred by the perceived lack of shareholder-centric governance practices.

3. Differences between Anglo-Saxon and Continental European Models of Corporate Governance

Building upon a thorough review of both models and drawing insights from several studies, notably the work of Gray et al. (2022), we elucidated in the following table the key differences between the Anglo-Saxon and the Continental European models across pivotal dimensions of corporate governance. These include ownership structure, managerial accountability, shareholder focus, regulatory environment, financial markets, the role of institutional investors, board structure and function, the role of banks, capital market accessibility, and approach to corporate social responsibility.

Table 1: Comparative Analysis of Corporate Governance Models: Anglo-Saxon vs. Continental European & Japan Approaches

Aspect	Anglo-Saxon Model	Continental European & Japan Model
Ownership Structure	Dominance of independent individuals and individual shareholders	Presence of stakeholder-oriented governance with significant influence from employees and other stakeholders
Managerial Accountability	Managers accountable to Board of Directors and shareholders	Managers accountable to a broader range of stakeholders, including employees and possibly government representatives
Shareholder Focus	Shareholders particularly interested in profitability and dividends	Shareholder interests extend beyond financial returns to include social and environmental concerns
Regulatory Environment	Regulatory focus on transparency, disclosure, and protection of shareholder rights	Regulatory emphasis on stakeholder representation, labor rights, and social responsibility
Financial Markets	Financial market activities dominate allocation of ownership and control rights	Financial market activities are important but balanced with stakeholder interests and long-term sustainability

Role of Institutional Investors	Institutional investors play a significant role, often holding substantial equity stakes	Institutional investors may have less influence compared to the Anglo-Saxon model, with more emphasis on long-term relationships
Board Structure and Function	Independent boards responsible for monitoring and improving organizational performance	Boards may include representatives from various stakeholder groups, with a focus on consensus-building and long-term sustainability
Role of Banks	Banks primarily viewed as credit providers, with less central role in governance structures	Banks may have more influence in governance, particularly in the German model, where bank representatives often sit on company boards
Capital Market Accessibility	High degree of capital dispersion, allowing widespread shareholder participation	Shareholder participation may be more limited, with emphasis on stability and long-term relationships
Approach to Corporate Social Responsibility	Focus on profitability and shareholder value, with CSR often seen as a means to enhance reputation	Integrated approach to CSR, with a focus on balancing the interests of multiple stakeholders and contributing to sustainable development

Source: Ungureanu, M. (2012). Models and practices of corporate governance worldwide. CES Working Papers, 4(3a), 625-635. Supplementary information was compiled from additional sources.

In light of this, it becomes evident that while both the Anglo-Saxon and Continental European models exhibit distinct approaches to corporate governance, each possesses its own set of strengths and weaknesses. Understanding these differences is crucial for policymakers, investors, and corporate leaders navigating the global business landscape. By recognizing the nuanced nuances between these models, stakeholders can make informed decisions to promote effective governance practices and sustainable business growth.

4. The corporate governance landscape in Algeria

The corporate governance landscape in Algeria has witnessed a growing interest and development in recent years. This evolution can be traced back to 2007, when the country hosted its first international conference on the subject of corporate governance (CG). This seminal event served as a platform for various stakeholders and interested parties in the Algerian business environment to convene and discuss the importance of CG.

One of the key outcomes of this conference was the crystallization of the idea to develop an "Algerian Charter for Good Governance for the company." This initiative was supported by the public authorities, particularly the Ministry of Small and Medium Enterprises, and brought together a diverse working group comprising representatives from international organizations, such as the International Finance Corporation and the Meda Program for the Development of Small and Medium Enterprises, as well as local organisations. The collaborative efforts of this multi-representative team culminated in the issuance of the Algerian Corporate Governance Charter in November 2009.

The Algerian Corporate Governance Charter was designed to serve as a practical guide and reference for companies in the country, drawing heavily on the principles of corporate governance established by the Organization for Economic Cooperation and Development (OECD). The charter aimed to provide a simplified and accessible framework for understanding and applying the fundamental principles of corporate governance, taking into account the unique characteristics and challenges faced by Algerian companies, particularly small and medium-sized enterprises.

This concerted effort to develop and promote corporate governance practices in Algeria represented a significant step forward in the country's quest to strengthen its institutional frameworks and promote more sustainable and accountable business practices. The introduction of the Algerian Corporate Governance Charter marked a qualitative leap towards the consolidation of governance practices in the country, signaling a growing recognition of the importance of good corporate governance for the long-term success and resilience of Algerian businesses.

While the Algerian Corporate Governance Charter represents an ambitious and commendable initiative, a closer examination of the charter and the broader corporate governance landscape in the country reveals several areas that warrant further attention and development.

One of the primary limitations of the charter is its primary focus on private small and medium-sized enterprises, while largely overlooking the governance needs of companies with public capital and those listed on the Algerian stock exchange. These latter categories of organizations, which are subject to heightened public accountability, lack a clear and comprehensive guidance framework to inform their corporate governance practices.

Additionally, the guidelines and principles outlined in the Algerian Charter, despite their practical orientation, are often characterized as being general and superficial in nature, lacking the depth and procedural specificity required to effectively guide companies in the implementation of sound corporate governance practices. This shortcoming suggests the need for more detailed and actionable guidance to be developed and disseminated to Algerian businesses.

Further compounding these challenges is the apparent lack of a dedicated institution or body tasked with the responsibility of overseeing, framing, and continuously upgrading the corporate governance practices in the country. Although the charter recommended the establishment of such a supporting entity, the materialization of this recommendation remains unclear, with no definitive evidence of its implementation.

These limitations are exacerbated by the broader contextual factors that shape the Algerian business and regulatory environment. The country's financial market is widely recognized as one of the weakest globally, with limited capacity to perform its role as a financial intermediary. Similarly, the Algerian banking system, despite recent reforms, continues to grapple with various systemic issues that undermine its ability to earn the trust and confidence of stakeholders.

Lastly, the Algerian context is characterized by a relative weakness and monopolization of state oversight and accountability mechanisms, with a notable absence of active and effective independent organizations that could complement and monitor the role of government regulatory bodies. This landscape poses significant challenges in ensuring the robust and impartial enforcement of corporate governance standards.

In light of these multifaceted challenges, the development of corporate governance in Algeria remains an ongoing process that requires a comprehensive and sustained effort to address the structural, institutional, and regulatory barriers hindering the effective implementation of sound governance practices across the country's diverse business landscape.

The development of corporate governance in Algeria must be viewed within the broader context of the country's evolving economic and regulatory landscape. While the introduction of the Algerian Corporate Governance Charter in 2009 represented a significant milestone, the challenges and limitations inherent in the charter and the surrounding ecosystem suggest the need for a more holistic and strategic approach to strengthening corporate governance practices in the country.

One of the primary areas recuiring attention is the expansion of the charter's scope and applicability. As previously noted, the current focus on private small and medium-sized enterprises, while important, overlooks the governance needs of larger, publicly-owned entities and those listed on the Algerian stock exchange. Developing comprehensive and tailored guidance for these organizations, which are subject to heightened public scrutiny and accountability, would be a crucial step in promoting more robust and transparent corporate governance practices across the entire business landscape.

Additionally, the identified need for more detailed and actionable guidelines within the Algerian Charter points to the importance of enhancing the depth and specificity of the principles and recommendations it provides. This would involve the development of clearer procedural frameworks, practical tools, and implementation strategies to assist Algerian companies in effectively translating the charter's guidelines into tangible governance practices.

The establishment of a dedicated institution or regulatory body to oversee, monitor and continuously update the corporate governance framework in Algeria also emerges as a critical priority. Such an entity would be responsible for providing guidance, facilitating knowledge-sharing, and ensuring the ongoing adaptation of governance standards to meet the evolving needs of Algerian businesses and the broader economic environment.

Addressing the broader contextual challenges, such as the weaknesses in the Algerian financial market and banking system, as well as the need for strengthening independent oversight and accountability mechanisms, will be crucial in creating an enabling environment for the effective implementation of corporate governance practices. Coordinated efforts involving policymakers, regulators, industry associations, and other stakeholders will be necessary to tackle these systemic issues and establish a more robust and supportive ecosystem for corporate governance.

By taking a comprehensive and strategic approach to strengthening corporate governance in Algeria, incorporating the expansion of guidance, the enhancement of implementation frameworks, the establishment of dedicated oversight institutions, and the reinforcement of the broader economic and regulatory infrastructure, the country can lay the foundation for more transparent accountable, and sustainable business practices – ultimately contributing to the long-term prosperity and competitiveness of Algerian enterprises.

However, beyond the considerations outlined earlier, there are several additional factors that should be taken into account to drive meaningful and sustainable progress in this domain.

One crucial aspect is the need to foster a cultural shift within the Algerian business community towards embracing the principles and practices of good corporate governance. This involves not only the dissemination of knowledge and awareness-raising efforts, but also the active engagement and buy-in of business leaders, entrepreneurs, and other key stakeholders. Highlighting the tangible benefits of effective corporate governance, such as enhanced access to capital, improved risk management, and stronger stakeholder relationships, can help catalyze this cultural transformation.

Closely linked to this is the imperative to strengthen the capacity and capabilities of Algerian institutions in implementing and sustaining sound corporate governance practices. This may involve the development of specialized training programs, the creation of professional development opportunities, and the facilitation of knowledge-sharing platforms that enable the exchange of best practices and lessons learned. Empowering Algerian businesses with the necessary skills, tools, and resources will be instrumental in driving the long-term adoption and institutionalization of corporate governance principles.

Moreover, the role of the Algerian government and regulatory authorities in shaping the corporate governance landscape cannot be overstated. Policymakers and regulators should consider the strategic deployment of incentives, mandates, and enforcement mechanisms to encourage and compel Algerian businesses to prioritize and implement robust governance structures. This could include the introduction of corporate governance codes, the establishment of listing requirements for publicly traded companies, and the strengthening of regulatory oversight and compliance frameworks.

Equally important is the need to foster greater collaboration and coordination among the various stakeholders involved in the corporate governance ecosystem in Algeria. This includes fostering stronger partnerships between the public and private sectors, facilitating the involvement of civil society organizations and academic institutions, and promoting cross-border cooperation and knowledge-sharing with international bodies and best practice-sharing networks. By aligning the efforts and resources of diverse stakeholders, a more cohesive and effective approach to corporate governance can be achieved.

Finally, the ongoing monitoring, evaluation, and iterative refinement of the corporate governance framework in Algeria will be crucial to ensuring its continued relevance and effectiveness in the face of evolving business dynamics and regulatory changes. Establishing robust data-gathering mechanisms, conducting regular assessments, and incorporating feedback from stakeholders will enable the continuous improvement and adaptation of the Algerian corporate governance landscape.

By addressing these multifaceted considerations, Algeria can work towards the development of a comprehensive and sustainable corporate governance system that not only strengthens the performance and resilience of its businesses, but also fosters greater transparency, accountability, and public trust in the country's economic and governance structures.

CHAPTER 5

CASE STUDIES AND SELF ASSESSMENT

Chapter 5: Case Studies and Self Assessment

In this chapter, we will explore two case studies involving two companies. Our objective is to provide readers with a comprehensive understanding of governance practices by examining published governance reports and annual reports from these companies. Through this case study, readers will gain insight into the practical application of theoretical concepts. Furthermore, we will offer a series of exercises encompassing diverse question types to facilitate self-assessment of the knowledge acquired from the various dimensions explored in this book.

To align with the study's methodology and its aim of informing readers on how to interpret governance reports and assess the level of governance practice within the company, we will focus our evaluation primarily on the Board of Directors and its committees. This will be done by addressing the following two key questions:

- Are the Board of Directors and its committees within the company adequately functioning, characterized by appropriate composition, independence, and size?
- Based on the findings, what recommendations can be proposed to enhance the functioning of the Board of Directors and its committees, addressing any identified imbalances?

To address these questions, we will assess the size, independence, and activity of both the Board of Directors and its committees using information available in the company's published governance report. Following this assessment, accompanied by thorough analysis, we will conclude with recommendations derived from the results obtained or conclusions reached.

1. The first case study: the British Telecom Group (BT Group plc)

BT Group plc is a leading British telecommunications company with a rich history dating back to the 19th century. Headquartered in London, United Kingdom, the company is one of the largest providers of fixed-line, mobile, and broadband services in the UK, serving both consumer and business customers. Operationally, BT Group is organized into four key business segments:

- **Consumer:** This division provides consumer fixed-line, broadband, and mobile services to households across the United Kingdom. It is a major player in the consumer telecommunications market, offering a range of bundled packages and innovative products.
- **Enterprise:** The Enterprise segment delivers a comprehensive suite of communications and IT services to businesses of all sizes, as well as the public sector. It supports organizations with their digital transformation and connectivity needs.
- **Global:** BT Group's Global division provides managed network and IT services to multinational corporations operating around the world. It leverages the company's extensive international infrastructure and expertise to serve large enterprise clients.
- **Openreach:** This division is responsible for managing and maintaining the UK's national broadband and telephone network infrastructure. Openreach plays a crucial role in ensuring reliable and ubiquitous connectivity across the country.

In the most recent financial year (FY2022), BT Group reported strong financial performance, with revenue of £21.3 billion and operating profit of £1.96 billion. The company also continued its commitment to shareholders, paying a dividend of 7.7 pence per share.

Having provided this overview of BT Group's business operations and financial highlights, the following sections will investigate a detailed assessment and analysis of the company's corporate governance practices, with a focus on the composition independence, and activities of its Board of Directors and key board committees. This assessment was made based on the corporate governance annual repor provided by the company in 2022.

1.1. BT Group's board of director

Table 2: BT Group's Board of Director Composition: Roles and Membership Types

Director	Roles	Nature of Membership
Adam Crozier	Independent	Chairman
Philip Jansen	Executive	Chief Executive
Simon Lowth	Executive	Chief Financial Officer
Adel Al-Saleh	Non-Independent	Non-Executive Director
Ian Cheshire	Independent	Non-Executive Director
Iain Conn	Independent	Senior Independent Director, Non-Executive Director
Isabel Hudson	Independent	Designated Non-Executive Director for Workforce Engagement, Non-Executive Director
Matthew Key	Independent	Non-Executive Director
Allison Kirkby	Independent	Non-Executive Director
Leena Nair	Independent	Non-Executive Director
Sara Weller	Independent	Non-Executive Director

Based on Table 2:

The Board comprises 11 members, consisting of 8 independent non-executive directors, 2 executive directors (CEO and CFO), and a Non-Independent director (Adel Al-Saleh):

- Adam Crozier holds the position of independent Chairman.
- Iain Conn serves as the Senior Independent Director.

- Isabel Hudson is designated as the Non-Executive Director for Workforce Engagement.

- **Board independence**

The level of board independence at BT Group plc can be calculated as the proportion of independent non-executive directors on the board:

Board Independence = Number of independent non-executive directors / Total number of directors

From the information provided, BT Group plc's board has 8 independent non-executive directors out of a total of 11 directors.

Board Independence = 8 / 11 = 72.72%

This indicates a high level of board independence, well above the UK Corporate Governance Code recommendation of at least 50% of the board, excluding the chair, being independent non-executive directors. The strong independence of the board enhances its ability to provide objective oversight and challenge to the executive management team.

- **Board Composition**

The report highlights the diversity of BT Group plc's board composition. Key metrics include:

- Gender Diversity: 4 out of 11 directors (36%) are female.
- Ethnic Diversity: 2 out of 11 directors (18%) are from ethnic minority backgrounds.
- Disability: 1 out of 11 directors (9%) has a disability.

These figures demonstrate that BT Group plc has made progress in achieving a diverse board composition, exceeding the 33% gender diversity target set by the Hampton-Alexander Review for FTSE 350 companies. The inclusion of directors from ethnic minority backgrounds and with disabilities also reflects the company's commitment to broader diversity and inclusion.

- **Board Size**

The BT Group plc board consists of 11 members, which is considered an appropriat size for a company of its scale and complexity. Although research often suggests tha boards with 8-10 members are typically the most effective for balancing divers perspectives with decision-making efficiency, a board of 11 members is stil acceptable and can provide a robust framework for oversight and governance.

- **Board Meeting Frequency**

The report indicates that the BT Group plc board held 9 scheduled meetings and 2 strategy meetings during the year, suggesting a regular cadence of board activities This meeting frequency appears to be towards the higher end of typical practic based on benchmarks and guidance. Academic research suggests 4-8 regular boar meetings per year is typical for large public companies, with more frequent meeting associated with companies facing greater challenges or undergoing strategic change In comparison, BT Group plc's 9 scheduled board meetings, supplemented by ar additional 2 strategy sessions, exceeds what is commonly observed in this research This high level of meeting frequency indicates a strong commitment by the B Group plc board to active oversight and governance of the company's operation and strategic direction.

1.2. Audit & Risk committee

Table 3: BT Group's Audit & Risk Committee: Member Roles and Membershi Nature

Member	Role	Nature of Membership
Matthew Key	Chair	Independent Non-Executive Director
Ian Cheshire	Member	Independent Non-Executive Director

Iain Conn	Member	Independent Non-Executive Director
Allison Kirkby	Member	Independent Non-Executive Director
Isabel Hudson	Member	Independent Non-Executive Director

- **Committee Size**

The Audit & Risk Committee at BT Group plc consists of 5 members. Academic literature suggests that audit committees of large public companies typically have between 3 to 7 members. A committee size of 5 is therefore considered appropriate, as it allows for sufficient expertise and oversight while maintaining effectiveness in decision-making and discussions.

- **Committee Independence**

Significantly, all 5 members of BT Group's Audit & Risk Committee are independent non-executive directors. This 100% independence level exceeds the recommendation in the UK Corporate Governance Code, which requires at least 3 independent non-executive directors on the audit committee. A fully independent audit committee is widely regarded as best practice, as it enhances the committee's ability to provide objective scrutiny and challenge to management.

- **Meeting Frequency**

The Audit & Risk Committee held 6 meetings during the year under review. Academic research suggests that audit committees of large public companies generally meet between 4 to 8 times per year. The 6 meetings held by BT Group's Audit & Risk Committee therefore fall within this typical range, indicating a robust cadence of activities. A higher frequency of meetings is often associated with companies facing greater challenges or undergoing significant changes, which may require more intensive oversight and monitoring by the committee.

1.3. Nominations Committee

Table 4: BT Group's Nominations Committee: Member Roles and Membership Nature

Member	Role	Nature of Membership
Adam Crozier	Chair	Independent Non-Executive Director (Chairman)
Ian Cheshire	Member	Independent Non-Executive Director
Iain Conn	Member	Independent Non-Executive Director
Sara Weller	Member	Independent Non-Executive Director

- **Committee Size**

The Nominations Committee at BT Group plc has 4 members. Prior research suggests that nominations committees typically range from 3 to 5 members, with larger boards tending to have larger nominations committees. A 4-member committee is therefore considered an appropriate size for a company of BT Group's scale and complexity.

- **Committee Independence**

All 4 members of the Nominations Committee are independent non-executive directors. This 100% independence level exceeds the recommendation in the UK Corporate Governance Code, which requires a majority of independent non-executive directors on the nominations committee. A fully independent nominations committee is regarded as best practice, as it helps ensure objectivity and fairness in the board nomination and succession planning process.

- **Meeting Frequency**

The Nominations Committee held 5 scheduled meetings during the year, with an additional 6 ad-hoc meetings. Academic studies on nominations committee activities suggest that larger public companies typically hold 4 to 8 meetings per year. The 11 total meetings held by BT Group's Nominations Committee, including the ad-hoc sessions, indicates a high level of engagement and diligence in fulfilling its responsibilities.

1.4. Remuneration Committee

Table 5: BT Group's Remuneration Committee: Member Roles and Membership Nature

Member	Role	Nature of Membership
Iain Conn	Member	Independent Non-Executive Director
Matthew Key	Member	Independent Non-Executive Director
Leena Nair	Member	Independent Non-Executive Director

- **Committee Size**

The Remuneration Committee has 3 members, which falls within the typical range of 3 to 5 members for board committees of large public companies.

- **Committee Independence**

All 3 members of the Remuneration Committee are independent non-executive directors, aligning with best practice recommendations. Independent oversight of executive remuneration is crucial for ensuring alignment with shareholders' interests.

- **Meeting Frequency**

The Remuneration Committee held 5 scheduled meetings, with an additional 3 ad hoc meetings. This frequency is consistent with academic research suggesting boar committees typically meet 4 to 8 times per year.

Overall, the evaluation of BT Group plc's board and committee structures independence, composition, and meeting cadence suggests the company ha implemented a corporate governance model that prioritizes accountability transparency, and effective oversight. This positions the organization well t navigate the challenges and opportunities ahead while protecting the interests of it shareholders and other stakeholders.

2. The second case study: Etisalat Group

Etisalat Group is a public joint stock company established in the UAE in 1976. It i one of the leading telecom groups in the Middle East, Africa and Asia, serving ove 149 million subscribers across 16 countries. The company's headquarters is locate in Abu Dhabi, UAE, with operations and subsidiaries in the UAE, Saudi Arabia Egypt, Pakistan, Morocco, Afghanistan, Sudan, Turkey, Pakistan, Afghanistan, Sr Lanka, Tanzania, South Africa, Benin, Ivory Coast and Niger.

Etisalat was founded in 1976, making it the first telecommunications company i the UAE. Over the years, the group has achieved several key milestones - it launche the first mobile network in the UAE in 1983, became the first telecom operator i the region to launch commercial 3G services in 1999, acquired a majority stake i Maroc Telecom in 2009 to expand its international presence, launched the UAE' first 4G LTE network in 2015, deployed the region's first 5G commercial network i 2018, and has been accelerating digital transformation initiatives across the Grou in recent years.

In 2017, Etisalat had a workforce of over 25,000 employees and provided comprehensive range of telecommunications services, including mobile, fixed broadband, TV, corporate, and wholesale. The company's strategic priorities wer focused on driving growth in core and new businesses, enhancing customer experience, maximizing operational efficiency, embracing digital transformation, and strengthening corporate culture and talent development.

Moreover, Etisalat's achievements have been widely recognized. The company has been ranked as the most valuable consumer brand in the MENA region by Brand Finance. Additionally, Etisalat has been awarded 'Platinum' status by the Sheikh Khalifa Excellence Award, recognized as 'Telecom Company of the Year' at the Gulf Business Awards, received the 'Best Digital Transformation Initiative' award at the CommsMEA Awards, and been awarded 'Best Operator' and 'Best Brand' at the World Communication Awards.

Drawing upon the corporate governance annual report of the Etisalat Group published in 2017, we will analyze the corporate governance practices of this company in the following section.

2.1. The board of director of Etisalat Group

Table 6: Etisalat Group's Board of Director Composition: Roles and Membership Types

Name	Membership Type	Role
Eissa Mohamed Ghanem Al Suwaidi	Non-Executive Independent	Chairman
Sheikh Ahmed Mohamed Soltan ben Sorour Al Dhaheri	Non-Executive Independent	Vice Chairman
Mohamed Sultan Abdulla Mohamed Al Hameli	Non-Executive Independent	Member
Abdulla Salem Obaid Salem Al Dhaheri	Non-Executive Independent	Member
Hisham Abdulla Qassim Al Qassim	Non-Executive Independent	Member
Eissa Abdul Fattah Kazim Al Molla	Non-Executive Independent	Member
Abdul Fattah El Said Mansour Sharaf	Non-Executive Independent	Member

Mohamed Hadi Ahmed Abdulla Al Hussaini	Non-Executive Independent	Member
Abdulmonem Bin Eisa Ben Naser Al Serkal	Non-Executive Independent	Member
Khalid Abdulwahid Hassan Al Rostamani	Non-Executive Independent	Member
Otaiba Khalaf Ahmed Khalef Al Otaiba	Non-Executive Independent	Member

- **Board independence**

From the above table, the level of independence of the board is 100 percent, which suggests that the board of directors is totally independent. While it's true that having a fully independent board, as indicated by the absence of executive members among the 11 board members, can enhance the board's independence from executive management, there are nuanced considerations to bear in mind.

Increasing the percentage of independent board members indeed strengthens the board's ability to monitor and oversee executive practices effectively. Moreover non-executive members typically bring diverse experiences and perspectives that can enrich board discussions and decision-making processes. They are expected to safeguard the interests of all stakeholders, not just shareholders.

However, it's important to recognize the valuable insights that executive members possess due to their direct involvement in the company's operations. Their familiarity with the company's activities and depth of experience can provide invaluable context during board deliberations.

While complete independence may seem advantageous, it could potentially lead to drawbacks. For instance, decisions made by a board comprised entirely of non-executive members might lack the practical insights and operational considerations that executive members can provide. This could impact the effectiveness of the board's decisions and their alignment with the company's strategic objectives.

Therefore, achieving a balance between independence and practical expertise is essential for optimal board performance. Incorporating a mix of independent and executive members ensures a diversity of perspectives while leveraging the valuable knowledge and experience of executive leadership. This approach fosters robust governance practices and enables informed decision-making that benefits all stakeholders.

- **The Size of the Board**

The Etisalat Group has structured its board of directors with 11 members, which aligns well with academic recommendations for effective corporate governance. The scholarly literature on board size indicates that boards comprising between 6 to 12 directors tend to strike a favorable balance - large enough to leverage a breadth of expertise and viewpoints, yet small enough to facilitate efficient decision-making and oversight responsibilities. The 11-member board of the ETISALAT Group appears to be well-suited to the scale and complexity of the organization based on these theoretical insights.

- **Board composition**

The Etisalat Group's board composition appears to lack diversity. Based on the information provided, the 11-member board consists entirely of members from the same gender and ethnic background, with 0% representation of diverse perspectives.

This lack of gender and ethnic diversity on the board is a concern from a corporate governance standpoint. Academic research has consistently demonstrated the benefits of diverse boards, including improved decision-making, enhanced risk management, and better alignment with the customer base and broader stakeholder interests. A homogeneous board composition can limit the breadth of skills, experiences, and viewpoints available to the organization.

2.2. The independence of the audit committee

Table 7: Etisalat Group's Audit Committee Composition

Name	Role
Eissa Abdul Fattah Kazim Al Molla	Chair
Sheikh Ahmed Mohamed Soltan ben Sorour Al Dhaheri	Member
Khalid Abdulwahid Hassan Al Rostamani	Member
Salem Soltan Al Dhaheri	External member

As the table shows, all four members of the committee are independent of the company's management. This independence is a crucial attribute, as it enables the committee members to exercise their discretion and judgment without undue influence from the executive team. With this independence, the Audit Committee is positioned to objectively assess the quality of the company's financial disclosures, the adequacy of its internal controls, and the avoidance of questionable management practices.

Moreover, the Audit Committee's composition is further enhanced by the presence of members, such as Al Molla and Al Rostamani, who possess knowledge and experience in accounting and finance. This specialized expertise allows the committee to conduct a thorough and informed evaluation of the company's financial reporting, internal controls, and risk management practices, ensuring that Etisalat Group's financial integrity and transparency are maintained.

Importantly, the Audit Committee also includes an external independent member who does not belong to the company's board of directors. The inclusion of this external perspective, independent of both management and the board, can bring an additional layer of objectivity and challenge to the committee's oversight responsibilities. This can help ensure that the committee's deliberations and recommendations are truly impartial and in the best interests of the company and its stakeholders.

2.3. The independence of the Nominations and Remuneration Committee

Table 8: Etisalat Group's Nominations and Remuneration Committee

Name	Role
Mohamed Sultan Abdulla Mohamed Al Hameli	Chair
Abdulla Salem Obaid Salem Al Dhaheri	Member
Hisham Abdulla Qassim Al Qassim	Member
Abdulmonem Bin Eisa Ben Naser Al Serkal	External member

The Etisalat Group's Nomination and Remuneration Committee is also noteworthy for being fully independent, with a 100% independent composition. This independent structure is a strength, as it allows the committee to nominate board members who are more likely to prioritize the interests of stakeholders over management's tendencies.

The independence of this committee is crucial, as it enables the committee to ensure that rewards and salaries are closely aligned with the company's actual performance. This can incentivize the executive management to work in the best interests of stakeholders in order to maximize their own compensation and retain their positions.

However, the absence of executive members on this committee means the perspective of management, who have the most intimate knowledge of the company's operations, is not directly represented. Management's input during the board nomination process and discussions around executive remuneration could be valuable, as they can provide insights into the realities and unique needs of the organization.

While the full independence of the Nomination and Remuneration Committee is a positive governance practice, the company may want to consider whether there is a way to incorporate the executive team's perspective in a balanced manner. This could involve, for example, allowing the executive management to provide input and feedback, while maintaining the committee's overall independence and decision-making authority.

2.4. Meeting Frequency

Table 9: Etisalat Group's Meeting Frequency per Year

	Meeting Frequency per year
Board of Directors	5
Audit Committee	8
The Nominations and Remuneration Committee	4

From the table provided, it is evident that the Etisalat Group's Board of Directors held 5 meetings during the period under review. This meeting frequency exceeds the legal minimum requirement of 4 meetings, indicating an active level of engagement by the Board in overseeing the company's operations and progress.

Furthermore, the Audit Committee convened 8 meetings, which is considerably more than the legal minimum. This high level of activity by the Audit Committee suggests a strong commitment to providing robust financial oversight and control. The frequent meetings enable the committee to closely scrutinize the company's financial reporting, internal controls, and risk management practices, thereby enhancing the overall integrity of the organization's financial management.

Regarding the Nomination and Remuneration Committee, the data shows that this committee held 4 meetings, which aligns with the recommended frequency of one meeting per semester. This meeting cadence can be considered a normal and acceptable level of activity, as it allows the committee to fulfill its responsibilities in a balanced manner, such as nominating new board members and reviewing executive compensation.

The differences in meeting frequencies across the various committees reflect their distinct roles and responsibilities within the Etisalat Group's corporate governance framework. While the Board of Directors' 5 meetings per year provide appropriate oversight and strategic guidance, the Audit Committee's heightened activity level of 8 meetings underscores its critical function in safeguarding the company's financial integrity. The Nomination and Remuneration Committee's 4 meetings per year represent a balanced approach to board composition and executive compensation matters.

2.5. Recommendations

Based on the results of the previous analysis, we conclude with the following recommendations:

- **Board Composition**
  - Consider introducing greater diversity, both in terms of gender and ethnicity, on the Board of Directors. This can inject new perspectives and enhance the board's decision-making capabilities.
  - Open the Board of Directors' membership to include executive members, with at least one-third of the board comprising executive members. This will ensure the continued independence of the majority, while allowing for the valuable input and perspectives of the executive team.
- **Board Committees**
  - Maintain the high level of activity and independence demonstrated by the Audit Committee, as this is a best practice in corporate governance.
  - Consider expanding the responsibilities of the Nomination and Remuneration Committee to include board succession planning and talent management, in addition to its current duties.
  - Open the membership of the Nomination and Remuneration Committee to include executive members, in the same one-third proportion recommended

for the Board of Directors. This will enable the committee to benefit from the executive team's insights and experiences.

- **Board Activities:**
  - Maintain the current frequency of 5 Board meetings per year, as this appears to strike a suitable balance between oversight and operational efficiency.
  - Encourage the Board to allocate sufficient time during meetings to review the progress of the company's strategic objectives, assess the performance of management, and provide guidance on key initiatives.
  - Implement a robust board evaluation process to identify areas for improvement in the Board's dynamics, decision-making, and overall effectiveness.
- **Transparency and Disclosure:**
  - Enhance the company's public disclosures related to the Board and its committees.
  - Provide more detailed information about the specific roles and responsibilities of the Board and each of its committees to improve stakeholder understanding of the governance framework.

3. Self Assessment

This section is designed to help you evaluate your understanding of corporate governance principles covered throughout the book. By engaging with these exercises, you can test your grasp of key concepts, reflect on their implications, and identify areas where further study might be beneficial. Each exercise is accompanied by solutions to guide you through the reasoning and expected outcomes, helping you consolidate your learning.

3.1. Exercises

Exercise 1:

- The Cadbury reports on the Financial Dimensions of Corporate Governance (1992) and "A Look at Corporate Governance" (1999) presented distinct definitions of the governance concept. Do these divergent definitions by Cadbury reflect agreement or disagreement among researchers on the concept of corporate governance?
- Governance is often conceptualized as a system comprising various components. Could you please list these components and provide an explanation for each?
- How does governance contribute to market efficiency?
- Is the concept of transparency synonymous with the concept of disclosure?. Please provide an explanation.
- Illustrate how the pursuit of fairness correlates with achieving the principles of governance.

Exercise 2:

Please indicate whether the following statements are true or false, and correct any errors if found.

- Corporate governance primarily aims to protect the interests of shareholders.
- Grey members do not have a contractual or non-contractual relationship or interest with the company and do not participate in its daily activities.
- The Audit Committee should convene with the rest of the Board members during their formal meetings at least four times a year.
- Audit services are among the costs of the obligation borne by the agent and the principal
- Increasing the number of internal members on the Board leads to a reduction in administrative opportunism.
- The high experience of members of audit committees leads to an increase in the reliability of disclosed information, resulting in a high level of information

asymmetry between the companies and stakeholders, ultimately leading to rationalized decisions.

Exercise 3:

Let's assume that an investor wanted to buy shares within Corporation X, and by analyzing the Corporation's governance report, he found the following:

- The CEO of the Corporation also serves as the Chairman of the Board of Directors.
- The Board of Directors consists of 10 members:
- 3 members are employees of Y Corporation, which conducts business for X Corporation in another country.
- 2 members are prominent figures within the local community associated with the Corporation.
- 2 members have no contractual relationship and possess expertise solely in financial and accounting matters.
- 3 members are employees of Corporation X.
- How would you assess the composition of the board in terms of independence? Please provide an explanation.
- Would you recommend that the investor purchase shares in the company? Why or why not?
- Do you believe the company could establish an audit committee? If so, what would be the composition of its members?

Exercise 4:

Please answer the questions below.

- Mathiesen Henrik defined corporate governance as "a system that aims to provide incentives to the company's management in order to improve its financial performance by providing an incentive mechanism that includes contracts, organizational plans, and regulations". Into which perspective does this definition fall, and could you provide an explanation?

- What arguments does agency theory offer in explaining the governance practices of an economic organization?

- Does the stakeholder agency theory provide a clear and robust explanation of corporate governance compared to the other two stakeholder theory perspectives?
- In what ways does board independence contribute to effective corporate governance?
- Explain how transparency leads to good corporate governance

Exercise 5:

Please indicate whether the following statements are true or false, and correct any errors if found:

- Stakeholder theory is somewhat vague but easy to apply.
- After the implementation of corporate governance, it has become easy to reach a contractual formula that completely prevents the existence of deviations by management.
- Audit committees are attached to executive management and their primary function is to ensure there is oversight of the board of directors.
- One of the strengths of concentrated ownership structures is that shareholders have an incentive to closely monitor the organization's activities.

Exercise 6:

Below is information about the composition of the board of directors of Jasmine, an Algerian company listed on the stock exchange operating in the plastic industry:

Table 10: Jasmine Company Board of Directors Composition: Roles and Affiliations

Member	Title	Affiliation/Background
Mr. Ahmed	Chairperson of the Council	Member of the Board of Directors of a service company.
Mr. Khalid	Member	Executive Director at the Jasmine company.
Mr. Mohsen	Member	Retired Accountant from the Public Sector (Retired 1 year ago)
Mr. Ali	Member	Consumer Protection Advocate
Mr. Farid	Member	Head of Purchasing Department

- Suppose an investor approached you for consultation on the efficiency of the governance system based on the provided data. Would you recommend investing or not?
- If you know that the company intends to form an audit committee, what composition do you deem most appropriate (Chairman and members), and could you explain your answer?

Exercise 7:

Please answer the questions below.

- Does Algeria possess the fundamental elements necessary to implement a corporate governance system based on OECD principles?
- Williamson noted that there can be no trust when a transaction is characterized by uncertainty. Why is this the case?
- Demonstrate how achieving accountability contributes to realizing the concept of governance.
- Does governance enhance the market value of shares?
- What is the overall importance of corporate governance?

Exercise 8:

Please indicate whether the following statements are true or false, and correct any errors if found.

- According to the managerial entrenchment theory, managers focus on projects directly related to the nature of their training or experience, provided that these projects are necessarily profitable for the company.
- Algeria has a clear guide for applying corporate governance that publicly accountable companies can follow.
- Unlike the Anglo-Saxon system, the Euro-Japanese system is characterized by the dispersion of ownership and its distribution among a large number of shareholders.
- The managerial perspective of stakeholder theory offers a clear explanation of corporate governance.
- The concept of governance is based on the full protection of the interests and rights of all stakeholders.

Exercise 9:

Here is the information about the composition of the board of directors of Green Algeria, an Algerian corporation listed on the stock exchange operating in the equipment industry for environmental protection:

Table 11: Green Algeria Corporation Board of Directors Composition: Roles and Affiliations

Member	Title	Affiliation/Background
Mr. Khalid	Member	Executive Director of the Green Algeria corporation
Mr. Ahmed	Member	Member of the Board of Directors of a service company

Mr. Mohsen	Member	Retired Accountant from the Public Sector (Retired 1 year ago)
Mr. Ali	Member	Consumer Protection Advocate
Mr. Farid	Member	Head of Purchasing Department

- Who do you believe is suitable for the position of Chairman of the Board, and why?
- If the individual you identified in your previous response as suitable for the position of Chairman of the Board were to hold that position, and an investor sought your advice on the efficiency of the governance system based on the provided data, would you recommend investing or not?
- If you were aware that the company intends to establish an audit committee what composition would you deem most appropriate (Chairman and members) and why?

3.2. Exercises solutions

Solution to Exercise 1:

- **The Cadbury reports on the Financial Dimensions of Corporate Governance (1992) and "A Look at Corporate Governance" (1999) presented distinct definitions of the governance concept. Do these divergent definitions by Cadbury reflect agreement or disagreement among researchers on the concept of corporate governance?**

Cadbury's definitions illustrate a noticeable difference in scholarly perspectives on governance. Initially outlined in 1992, Cadbury's portrayal of governance was limited to protecting shareholders' interests and optimizing the financial performance of the organization. However, in its subsequent definition in 1999 Cadbury's understanding of governance expanded to include safeguarding the interests of stakeholders. Additionally, it incorporated broader considerations, such as social objectives, alongside economic goals, aiming to balance the needs of the company with those of society. As a result, Cadbury's 1992 definition aligned with a more traditional, narrow view of governance, whereas its 1999 definition embraced a broader understanding, acknowledging the diverse aspects of corporate governance.

- **Governance is often conceptualized as a system comprising various components. Could you please list these components and provide an explanation for each?**

The components of the governance system are:

System Inputs: Legal, economic, financial, social, and ethical requirements stemming from the provision of resources to the company Delegation of authority to management as per contractual terms

Processing: Addressing these requirements or managing these elements. Oversight by internal parties such as the board of directors, board committees, and internal auditors. Involvement of external parties such as financial markets, government/professional bodies, and external auditors. Grounded in ethical conduct, control mechanisms, and risk management practices.

System Outputs: Safeguarding the interests of the company's stakeholders, including shareholders, lenders, customers, employees, and society at large. Achieved within a framework of accountability, fairness, disclosure, and transparency

- **How does governance contribute to market efficiency?**

Effective governance facilitates the dissemination of pertinent information to investors, enabling them to enhance their understanding of companies' performance, ascertain the implementation status of corporate strategies, and assess risk management measures. Consequently, well-informed investors are empowered to allocate their funds to promising ventures and better-managed enterprises, thereby fostering efficient market dynamics.

- **Is the concept of transparency synonymous with the concept of disclosure? Please provide an explanation.**

No, the concept of transparency is not synonymous with the concept of disclosure. Transparency pertains to the clarity and openness of a company's actions to external parties, contrasting with confidentiality, which involves intentional concealment of actions. Transparency involves removing the veil from intentionally hidden actions. On the other hand, disclosure refers to the provision of information to the public, irrespective of its accuracy, completeness, relevance, or timeliness. While disclosure entails making information available, even if it is incomplete or does not fully reflect the company's actual situation, this practice falls short of achieving transparency.

In essence, transparency goes beyond mere disclosure by not only making information available but also ensuring that it is comprehensive, accurate, relevant, and timely, thereby allowing external parties to gain a clear understanding of the company's actions and operations.

- **Illustrate how the pursuit of fairness correlates with achieving the principles of governance.**

The pursuit of fairness is intrinsically linked to achieving the principles of governance. Fairness involves balancing the interests of stakeholders within a company in a manner that upholds their rights and prevents bias towards any party. When a company strives to balance the interests of its stakeholders and safeguard their rights, it inherently aligns with the core principles of governance. Governance encompasses the processes and structures through which decisions are made and implemented to achieve organizational objectives while considering the needs and rights of all stakeholders.

By prioritizing fairness, companies ensure that the interests of stakeholders are protected and met equitably. This commitment to fairness not only fosters trust and confidence among stakeholders but also enhances the institution's overall effectiveness and sustainability.

Solution to Exercise 2:

Please indicate whether the following statements are true or false, and correct any errors if found:

- **Corporate governance primarily aims to protect the interests of shareholders.**

The statement is **true**. Corporate governance indeed primarily aims to protect the interests of shareholders.

- **Grey members do not have a contractual or non-contractual relationship or interest with the company and do not participate in its daily activities.**

The statement is **false**. "Grey members" are typically individuals or entities who have some level of involvement or association with an organization, albeit not as formalized as contractual or non-contractual relationships. They may not participate in the company's daily activities to the same extent as other members, but they often have some level of engagement or interest in the organization's affairs.

- **The Audit Committee should convene with the rest of the Board members during their formal meetings at least four times a year.**

The statement is **true**. Typically, the Audit Committee, as part of its responsibilities, meets regularly with the rest of the Board members during formal meetings. These meetings are usually scheduled quarterly, which means at least four times a year. This frequency allows for comprehensive discussions on financial reporting, internal controls, audit findings, and other matters pertinent to the committee's oversight role.

- **Audit services are among the costs of the obligation borne by the agent and the principal**

The statement is **false**. Audit services are typically incurred by the principal (the company or organization) rather than by the agent. The principal bears the responsibility for ensuring accurate financial reporting and compliance with relevant regulations, and therefore, it covers the costs associated with auditing services. The agent, on the other hand, may be involved in facilitating the audit process as necessary, but the ultimate obligation and cost usually lie with the principal.

- **Increasing the number of internal members on the Board leads to a reduction in administrative opportunism.**

The statement is **false**. Increasing the number of internal members on the Board generally does not increase independence and thus does not typically lead to a reduction in management opportunism. Internal members, such as executives or managers within the organization, may have inherent conflicts of interest due to their roles and affiliations. Their loyalty may be more aligned with management objectives rather than shareholder interests, potentially limiting their ability to provide objective oversight.

In contrast, increasing the number of independent or external members on the Board is more likely to enhance independence and reduce administrative opportunism. Independent directors, who are not affiliated with the organization or its management, can provide unbiased perspectives and act as a check on managerial decisions, thereby reducing the risk of opportunistic behavior.

Therefore, while internal members may contribute valuable insights and expertise, increasing the proportion of independent members is generally considered more effective in promoting governance integrity and mitigating administrative opportunism.

- **The high experience of members of audit committees leads to an increase in the reliability of disclosed information, resulting in a high level of information asymmetry between the company and stakeholders, ultimately leading to rationalized decisions.**

The statement is false. The high experience of members of audit committees generally leads to an increase in the reliability of disclosed information. This enhanced reliability typically reduces the level of information asymmetry between the company and stakeholders. When information provided by the company is more accurate and trustworthy, stakeholders have a clearer understanding of the organization's financial health, performance, and risks. Consequently, rationalized decisions can be made based on a more informed assessment of the available information, ultimately fostering greater trust and confidence among stakeholders. Therefore, it's more accurate to state that increased experience among audit committee members results in a reduction, rather than an increase, in the level of information asymmetry.

Solution to Exercise 3:

Let's assume that an investor wanted to buy shares within Corporation X, and by analyzing the Corporation's governance report, he found the following:

- The CEO of the corporation also serves as the Chairman of the Board of Directors.
- The Board of Directors consists of 10 members:
    - 3 members are employees of Y Corporation, which conducts business for X Corporation in another country.
    - 2 members are prominent figures within the local community associated with the corporation.
    - 2 members have no contractual relationship and possess expertise solely in financial and accounting matters.
    - 3 members are employees of Corporation X.

- **How would you assess the composition of the board in terms of independence? Please provide an explanation.**

In this scenario, the lack of independence is evident due to the CEO also serving as the Chairman of the Board of Directors. When the CEO holds the position of Chairman, there is a potential concentration of power and influence, as the same individual is responsible for both executive management and board leadership roles. This duality may compromise the board's ability to effectively monitor and challenge management decisions, as there could be a reluctance to question or challenge the CEO's actions.

Additionally, the presence of a significant number of "grey members," who typically lack formal affiliations or contractual relationships with the organization, further raises concerns about independence. In this case, with only four independent members out of ten total members on the board, there is a lack of diversity and a potential overrepresentation of executives or individuals closely associated with the organization's management.

Specifically, out of the 10 board members:

- 3 members are classified as "grey members".
- Additionally, there are 3 executive members.

This means that a total of 6 out of 10 members on the board are executives indicating a significant presence of non-independent members closely associated with the organization's management.

Overall, the composition of the board appears to lack sufficient independence, with only 40% of the board members being independent. This imbalance can undermine the board's effectiveness in providing impartial oversight and safeguarding the interests of shareholders and other stakeholders. To enhance independence, it may be advisable to appoint an independent Chairman separate from the CEO and to increase the proportion of independent directors on the board. These measures can help mitigate conflicts of interest and promote greater accountability and transparency in corporate governance

- **Would you recommend that the investor purchase shares in the company? Why or why not?**

Based on the information provided about the lack of independence on the board, particularly with the CEO also serving as Chairman and the majority of members being non-independent executives, there are concerns about corporate governance practices within the company. These governance issues could potentially impact transparency, accountability, and decision-making processes, which may in turn affect the institution's financial performance and long-term sustainability.

Investors typically value companies with strong corporate governance practices, as they are associated with better risk management, ethical conduct, and long-term value creation. In this case, the lack of independence on the board raises red flags about potential conflicts of interest and the adequacy of oversight mechanisms.

Therefore, without further information or assurances that the company is taking steps to address governance concerns and improve board independence, it may not be advisable for the investor to purchase shares in the institution at this time. It would be prudent for the investor to conduct further due diligence and consider alternative investment opportunities with stronger governance frameworks.

- **Do you believe the company could establish an audit committee? If so, what would be the composition of its members?**

Yes, they can form an audit committee. One of the conditions that must be met in the audit committee is the presence of at least 3 members of the board, preferably independent and experienced in financial and accounting matters, without it being a condition on which the formation of the committee depends. Accordingly, the committee members will consist of 2 independent members with expertise in financial and accounting matters and one member from the local community if the law requires independence in the formation of the committee. If the independence requirement is not met, a member will be added to the committee, even if they are a grey or executive member, and here they will be differentiated based on the proximity of their qualifications or experience to financial and accounting matters.

Solution to Exercise 4:

Please answer the questions below

- **Mathiesen Henrik defined corporate governance as "a system that aims to provide incentives to the company's management in order to improve its financial performance by providing an incentive mechanism that includes contracts, organizational plans, and regulations". Into which perspective does this definition fall, and could you provide an explanation?**

The perspective presented in Mathiesen Henrik's definition aligns more closely with the narrow view of corporate governance.

Focus on Financial Performance: The definition emphasizes improving the company's financial performance as the primary goal of corporate governance. This narrow focus prioritizes shareholder value maximization and tends to overlook other dimensions of governance, such as social responsibility or stakeholder interests.

Incentive Mechanism for Management: The definition highlights the role of incentive mechanisms, such as contracts and organizational plans, in motivating management to enhance financial performance. This approach primarily concerns itself with the agency problem between shareholders and management and seeks to address it through economic incentives.

Emphasis on Regulations: While regulations are mentioned as part of the incentive mechanism, they are primarily seen as a tool to enforce contractual agreements and ensure compliance, rather than as a means to promote broader social or ethical objectives.

- **What arguments does agency theory offer in explaining the governance practices of an economic organization?**

Agency theory posits that the separation of ownership from management, along with the divergence of interests between principals (owners) and agents (managers), gives rise to agency problems, including moral hazard and conflicting choices. To mitigate these issues and align the interests of both parties, organizations incur agency costs, which manifest as a set of procedures encompassing compliance, supervision, and monitoring. These costs are borne by the organization and are aimed at ensuring managerial actions are in the best interests of shareholders or lenders, thereby constituting governance mechanisms.

- **Does the stakeholder agency theory provide a clear and robust explanation of corporate governance compared to the other two stakeholder theory perspectives?**

Stakeholder agency theory recognizes the influential power of stakeholders, and it also recognizes the self-interested utilitarian orientation of the parties to the contract. By recognizing the self-interested utilitarian orientation of the parties to the contract, it opens the way for the search to find ways to protect their interests, which explains the need for governance mechanisms to protect the interests of stakeholders, unlike the two previous perspectives. The normative perspective sees the organization as accountable to all stakeholders, making it in fact and ultimately accountable to no one. The managerial perspective calls for balancing the needs of stakeholders, focusing on how an organization can identify its stakeholders and their needs, without answering how stakeholders can protect their interests.

- **In what ways does board independence contribute to effective corporate governance?**

Here are several ways in which board independence contributes to effective corporate governance:

Objective Oversight: Independent directors are not affiliated with the company' management, allowing them to provide impartial and objective oversight. They ca critically evaluate management's decisions and actions without bias, ensuring tha the interests of shareholders and other stakeholders are prioritized.

Enhanced Accountability: Independent directors hold managemen accountable for their actions and performance. Their independence enables them t ask tough questions, challenge management's assumptions, and deman accountability for the company's strategic direction and operational performance.

Alignment with Shareholder Interests: Independent directors represent th interests of shareholders and serve as their voice in the boardroom. Their primar duty is to protect shareholder value and ensure that management's actions ar aligned with the long-term interests of shareholders.

Risk Management: Independent directors bring diverse expertise an perspectives to the board, including experience in risk management. They play critical role in identifying and mitigating risks that may threaten the company' reputation, financial stability, or strategic objectives.

Effective Governance Structures: Independent directors often lead key boar committees, such as the audit, compensation, and nominating committees. Thei leadership ensures that these committees operate effectively, uphold best practices and fulfill their oversight responsibilities.

Stakeholder Confidence: The presence of independent directors instill confidence among investors, stakeholders, and regulatory authorities. It signals tha the company is committed to sound corporate governance practices, transparency and ethical behavior.

Legal and Regulatory Compliance: Independent directors help ensure that th company complies with applicable laws, regulations, and corporate governanc guidelines. Their oversight helps mitigate legal and regulatory risks and reduces th likelihood of corporate scandals or governance failures.

- **Explain how transparency leads to good corporate governance**

Transparency means providing the information that stakeholders need to make decisions, the absence of which leads to misinformation and thus harms their interests and rights. Since the concept of governance is based on the goal of protecting the interests of stakeholders, achieving transparency in the organization's practices necessarily means achieving the concept of governance.

Solution to Exercise 5:

Please indicate whether the following statements are true or false, and correct any errors if found:

- **Stakeholder theory is somewhat vague but easy to apply.**

The statement is **False**. Stakeholder theory is not necessarily vague but can be complex to apply due to the diverse interests and relationships among stakeholders. It involves identifying and prioritizing the needs and concerns of various stakeholders, which can be challenging in practice. Additionally, stakeholders' interests may evolve over time, requiring ongoing assessment and adaptation of strategies to effectively address their needs. Therefore, while stakeholder theory provides a valuable framework for understanding the broader impact of business decisions, its application may require careful consideration and nuanced approaches.

- **After the implementation of corporate governance, it has become easy to reach a contractual formula that completely prevents the existence of deviations by management.**

The statement is **False**. While corporate governance frameworks aim to reduce deviations by management and improve accountability, it is unrealistic to expect that any contractual formula can completely prevent all deviations. Management may still engage in unethical behavior or make poor decisions despite governance mechanisms in place. Corporate governance serves to mitigate risks and provide oversight, but it cannot eliminate all possibilities of deviations. Continuous monitoring, evaluation, and adaptation of governance practices are necessary to address emerging challenges and ensure effective governance over time.

- **Audit committees are attached to executive management and their primary function is to ensure there is oversight of the board of directors.**

The statement is **False**. Audit committees are typically independent bodies within an organization, separate from executive management. Their primary function is to provide oversight of the financial reporting process, internal controls, and audit activities. While they report to the board of directors, their independence from executive management ensures impartiality and effectiveness in their oversight role

- **One of the strengths of concentrated ownership structures is that shareholders have an incentive to closely monitor the organization's activities.**

The statement is **True**. In concentrated ownership structures, where a small number of shareholders hold significant stakes in the company, shareholders often have a stronger incentive to closely monitor the organization's activities. Because their financial interests are directly tied to the performance and behavior of the company, they are more likely to actively engage in monitoring management decisions, financial performance, and corporate governance practices. This can lead to better alignment of interests between shareholders and management, increased accountability, and improved corporate performance.

Solution to Exercise 6:

Based on the information detailed in Table 10, we will address the following questions:

- **Suppose an investor approached you for consultation on the efficiency of the governance system based on the provided data. Would you recommend investing or not?**

We advise the investor to consider investing. The presence of a majority of external independent members (Mr. Ahmed, Mohsen, Ali) compared to internal members (Mr. Khalid, Farid) suggests a level of board independence that could help mitigate bias towards management and minimize managerial opportunism.

- **If you know that the company intends to form an audit committee, what composition do you deem most appropriate (Chairman and members), and could you explain your answer?**

Based on the provided criteria and considering the need for independence and expertise in financial matters, the recommended composition for the audit committee of Jasmine would be:

Chairman:

Mr. Mohsen: Given his experience in accounting and financial matters, Mr. Mohsen is suitable to serve as the chairman of the committee.

Members:

Mr. Ali: As an independent member, Mr. Ali can provide unbiased oversight and contribute to the committee's independence.

Mr. Farid: Head of the Purchasing Department and possessing expertise in financial matters due to his position, Mr. Farid can bring valuable insights and perspective to the committee.

This composition ensures that the audit committee consists of at least three members, as recommended, and maintains a balance between independence and expertise in financial matters. Mr. Mohsen's chairmanship, along with the inclusion of an independent member (Mr. Ali) and an executive member with financial expertise (Mr. Farid), meets the legal requirements and ensures effective oversight of financial reporting and audit activities within the organization.

Solution to Exercise 7:

Please answer the questions below.

- **Does Algeria possess the fundamental elements necessary to implement a corporate governance system based on OECD principles?**

Algeria faces significant challenges in implementing a corporate governance system based on OECD principles. While the Algerian Charter of Good Governance acknowledges the OECD principles as its main reference, the fundamental elements necessary for effective corporate governance are lacking in the Algerian environment.

Weak Financial Market: The financial market in Algeria is described as one of the weakest globally and is unable to fulfill its role as a financial intermediary effectively. This weakness undermines investor confidence and hinders the functioning of capital markets, which are essential for corporate governance.

Banking System Issues: Despite witnessing reforms, the banking system in Algeria continues to face significant problems. It lacks the confidence expected from it, especially due to issues such as accumulated deficits inherited from public companies and the weakness and monopoly of state control and accountability mechanisms.

Absence of Independent Oversight Bodies: There is a near absence of active and effective local independent organizations or bodies that can complement and monitor the role of government oversight and accountability bodies. This lack of independent oversight further weakens corporate governance practices.

- **Williamson noted that there can be no trust when a transaction is characterized by uncertainty. Why is this the case?**

Because of the impossibility of reaching a perfect contract between all individuals that takes into account all current and future variables and leaves no room for coincidences that could affect the rights of all contracting parties. Therefore, it is necessary to establish monitoring and follow-up systems that are agreed upon during the contract and also after the contract whenever the need arises.

- **Demonstrate how achieving accountability contributes to realizing the concept of governance.**

Accountability ensures that stakeholders have the necessary information and transparency to understand management's actions and practices. By holding management accountable, stakeholders can make informed decisions about their involvement with the organization, thereby safeguarding their interests. This aligns with the core principle of governance, which is primarily concerned with protecting the interests of stakeholders. Ultimately, accountability promotes trust, transparency, and integrity within the organization, contributing to its overall effectiveness and sustainability.

- **Does governance enhance the market value of shares?**

Investors prefer to invest their money in companies that have a good governance structure because companies without good governance structures are more likely to risk financial failure or embezzlement than others due to their weak control and accounting systems, so companies without governance structures have limited access to financing in international markets and vice versa. This results in maximizing the market value of the organization as investors are willing to buy the company's shares and further attract investments.

- **What is the overall importance of corporate governance?**

The importance of governance can be summarized in that it helps to achieve the concept of sustainable development, i.e. reaching the needs of the present generation without sacrificing or harming the ability of future generations to meet their needs. Governance drives the maximization of an organization's economic performance, while taking into account social and environmental requirements within a framework of ethical values and principles.

Solution to Exercise 8:

Please indicate whether the following statements are true or false, and correct any errors if found.

- **According to the managerial entrenchment theory, managers focus on projects directly related to the nature of their training or experience, provided that these projects are necessarily profitable for the company.**

The statement is **False**. According to the managerial entrenchment theory managers focus on projects that are directly related to their training or experience even if these projects are not necessarily profitable for the organization.

- **Algeria has a clear guide for applying corporate governance that publicly accountable companies can follow.**

The statement is **False**. The guide, which takes the form of a charter, is primarily aimed at private SMEs, and excludes from its application both publicly traded and publicly accountable organizations.

- **Unlike the Anglo-Saxon model, the Euro-Japanese model is characterized by the dispersion of ownership and its distribution among a large number of shareholders.**

The statement is **False.** Unlike the Anglo-Saxon model, the Euro-Japanese model is characterized by the concentration of ownership in the hands of a few individuals with the dominance of institutional investors and banks, and the relationships between investors and companies are characterized by the search for continuity and permanence.

- **The managerial perspective of stakeholder theory offers a clear explanation of corporate governance.**

The statement is **False.** The managerial perspective of stakeholder theory does not address how stakeholders protect their interests.

- **The concept of governance is based on the full protection of the interests and rights of all stakeholders.**

The statement is **True**. The concept of governance is indeed based on the full protection of stakeholders' interests and rights. Governance practices aim to ensure that the interests and rights of stakeholders, including shareholders, employees, customers, suppliers, and the broader community, are safeguarded and considered in organizational decision-making processes. Effective governance involves transparency, accountability, fairness, and ethical conduct, all of which contribute to protecting the interests of stakeholders and promoting long-term sustainability and value creation for the organization.

Solution to Exercise 9:

Based on the information detailed in Table 11, we will address the following questions:

- **Who do you believe is suitable for the position of Chairman of the Board, and why?**

The right person for the chairman position is Mr. Ahmed. He is independent and has experience in leading a board of directors at another organization.

If the individual you identified in your previous response as suitable for the position of Chairman of the Board were to hold that position, and an investor sought your advice on the efficiency of the governance system based on the provided data, would you recommend investing or not?

Given that the Board of Directors enjoys independence, with 3 independen members compared to 2 non-independent members, and considering th separation between management and control functions, along with the Chairman c the Board's previous management experience, I would recommend investing Additionally, the diversity in the experience of the Board members to some exten further supports this recommendation.

- **If you were aware that the company intends to establish an audi committee, what composition would you deem most appropriat (Chairman and members), and why?**

For the Audit Committee, the most appropriate composition would be:

Chairman: Mr. Mohsen, chosen for his independence and experience i accounting and financial matters.

Members: Mr. Ali, selected for his independence, and Mr. Farid, an executiv member with experience in financial matters and familiarity with interna operations.

This composition ensures a balance of independence and expertise within the Audi Committee, enabling effective oversight of financial reporting and internal controls

REFERENCES

REFERENCES

AccountAbility. (1999). AccountAbility 1000 (AA1000) framework, standards, guidelines and professional qualification. Exposure draft. The Institute of Social and Ethical Accountability.

Aburaya, R. K. (2012). The relationship between corporate governance and environmental disclosure: UK evidence [Doctoral dissertation, Durham University].

Al-Lawzi, S. M. M. (2014). Hukumat al-'alaqah bayna atraf al-'aqd fi al-masrif al-'islamiyah 'ala dhou' mabda' al-'adalah: 'Aqd al-mudarabah namudhajan [Doctoral dissertation, World Islamic Sciences and Education University].

Al-Wasmi, M. E. (2011). Corporate governance practice in the GCC: Kuwait as a case study [Doctoral dissertation, Brunel University].

Alves, H. S. A. (2011). Corporate governance determinants of voluntary disclosure and its effects on information asymmetry: An analysis for Iberian Peninsula listed companies [Doctoral dissertation, University of Coimbra].

Andreadakis, S. (2010). Corporate governance in the aftermath of the scandals: The EU response and the role of ethics [Doctoral dissertation, University of Leicester].

Basel Committee on Banking Supervision. (2015). Corporate governance principles for banks. https://www.bis.org/bcbs/publ/d328.htm

Bourne, L. (2005). Project relationship management and the stakeholder circle [Doctoral dissertation, RMIT University].

BT Group. (n.d.). *Annual reports*. BT. https://www.bt.com/about/investors/financial-reporting-and-news/annual-reports

Bushman, R. M., Piotroski, J. D., & Smith, A. J. (2004). What determines corporate transparency? Journal of Accounting Research, 42(2), 207-252.

Cadbury, A. (1992). The financial aspects of corporate governance. https://www.icaew.com/library/subject-gateways/corporate-governance/codes-and-reports/cadbury-report

Cadbury A (1999) "Foreword," in World Bank report. In: Corporate governance: a framework for implementation – overview. Work Bank, Washington, DC. https://documents1.worldbank.org/curated/pt/831651468781818619/pdf/30446.pdf

Center for International Private Enterprise. (2002). Instituting corporate governance in developing, emerging and transitional economies: A handbook.

Chabuka, C. M. (2008). Corporate governance best practice: A case study of Copperbelt privately owned mining establishments [Master's thesis, The Copperbelt University].

Chan, M. C. C. (2010). The impact of corporate governance and firm characteristics on the voluntary disclosure of corporate social responsibility information: Australian evidence [Doctoral dissertation, University of Western Australia].

Charreaux, G. (2002). Quelle théorie pour la gouvernance? De la gouvernance actionnariale à la gouvernance cognitive [Working paper].

Clemente, A. G., & Labat, B. N. (2009). Corporate governance mechanisms and voluntary disclosure: The role of independent directors in the boards of listed Spanish firms. Universidad Autonoma de Madrid.

Cormier, D., Ledoux, M. J., Magnan, M., & Aerts, W. (2010). Corporate governance and information asymmetry between managers and investors. Corporate Governance: The International Journal of Business in Society, 10(5), 574-589.

Demirag, I., Sudarsanam, S., & Wright, M. (2000). Corporate governance: Overview and research agenda. British Accounting Review, 32(4), 341-354.

Donaldson, T., & Preston, L. E. (1995). The stakeholder theory of the corporation: Concepts, evidence, and implications. Academy of Management Review, 20(1), 65-91.

Duztas, S. (2008). Corporate governance: The effects of board characteristics, information technology maturity and transparency on company [Doctoral dissertation, Yeditepe University].

Etisalat Group. (n.d.). Annual reports. eand. https://www.eand.com/en/investors/annual reports.html

Executive Board of the United Nations Development Programme and of the United Nations Population Fund. (2008). The UNDP accountability system: Accountability framework and oversight policy (DP/2008/16/Rev.1). United Nations Development Programme. https://digitallibrary.un.org/record/635249/files/DP_2008_16_Rev1-EN.pdf

Fauzi, F., & Locke, S. (2012). Board structure, ownership structure and firm performance: A study of New Zealand listed-firms. Asian Academy of Management Journal of Accounting and Finance, 8(2), 43-67.

Financial Reporting Council. (n.d.). *UK Corporate Governance Code*. Financial Reporting Council. https://www.frc.org.uk/library/standards-codes-policy/corporate-governance/uk-corporate-governance-code/

Florini, A. (Ed.). (2007). The right to know: Transparency for an open world. Columbia University Press.

Freeman, R. E. (1984). Strategic management: A stakeholder approach. Pitman.

Fung, B. (2014). The demand and need for transparency and disclosure in corporate governance. Universal Journal of Management, 2(2), 72-80.

Ghabayen, M. A. (2012). Board characteristics and firm performance: Case of Saudi Arabia. International Journal of Accounting and Financial Reporting, 2(2), 168-200.

Gregory, H. J., & Simms, M. E. (1999, October 10-15). Corporate governance: What it is and why it matters [Conference presentation]. 9th International Anti-Corruption Conference, Durban, South Africa.

Hayes, R., Mehran, H., & Schaefer, S. (2004). Board committee structures, ownership and firm performance [Unpublished manuscript]. Federal Reserve Bank of New York.

Heenetigala, K. (2011). Corporate governance practices and firm performance of listed companies in Sri Lanka [Doctoral dissertation, Victoria University].

Hermanson, D. R., & Rittenberg, L. E. (2003). Internal audit and organizational governance. In A. D. Bailey, A. A. Gramling, & S. Ramamoorti (Eds.), Research opportunities in internal auditing (pp. 25-71). The Institute of Internal Auditors Research Foundation.

Hill, C. W. L., & Jones, T. M. (1992). Stakeholder-agency theory. Journal of Management Studies, 29(2), 131-154.

Hill, C., & Crombie, N. (2010, July 11-13). Accountability to stakeholders in a student-managed organisation [Conference presentation]. 6th Asia Pacific Interdisciplinary Research in Accounting Conference, Sydney, Australia.

Hussainey, K., & Salama, A. (2010). The importance of corporate environmental reputation to investors. Journal of Applied Accounting Research, 11(3), 229-241.

Ibn Manzur, M. (n.d.). Lisan al-'Arab (Vol. 11). Dar Sadir.

Iskander, M., & Chamlou, N. (2000). Corporate governance: A framework for implementation - Overview. The World Bank Group.

John, K., & Senbet, L. W. (1998). Corporate governance and board effectiveness. Journal of Banking & Finance, 22(4), 371-403.

Keasey, K., & Wright, M. (1993). Issues in corporate accountability and governance: An editorial. Accounting and Business Research, 23(sup1), 291-303.

Keong Low, C. (2002). Corporate governance: An Asia-Pacific critique. Sweet & Maxwell Asia.

Lipton, M., & Lorsch, J. W. (1992). A modest proposal for improved corporate governance. The Business Lawyer, 48(1), 59-77.

Madhani, P. M. (2015). Study of relationship between board committees and corporate governance practices of Indian firms. Global Management Review, 9(3), 1-21.

Mathiesen, H. (2002). Managerial ownership and finance performance [Doctoral dissertation, Copenhagen Business School].

Mosunova, N. (2014). The content of accountability in corporate governance. Russian Law Journal, 2(3), 116-139.

Ness, K. E., & Mirza, A. M. (1991). Corporate social disclosure: A note on a test of agency theory. The British Accounting Review, 23(3), 211-217.

Organisation for Economic Co-operation and Development. (2004). OECD principles of corporate governance. OECD Publishing.

Patten, D. M., & Crampton, W. (2003). Legitimacy and the internet: An examination of corporate web page environmental disclosures. In S. Sharma & M. Starik (Eds.), Advances in Environmental Accounting & Management (Vol. 2, pp. 31-57). Emerald Group Publishing Limited.

Puni, A. (2015). Do board committees affect corporate financial performance? Evidence from listed companies in Ghana. International Journal of Business and Management Review, 3(5), 71-88.

Rachid, K., & Islam, S. M. N. (2008). Corporate governance and firm value: Econometric modelling and analysis of emerging and developed financial markets. In K. V. Thai, D. Rahm, & J. D. Coggburn (Eds.), Handbook of Globalization and the Environment (pp. 439-478). CRC Press.

Rezaee, Z. (2009). Corporate governance and ethics. John Wiley & Sons.

Shankman, N. A. (1999). Reframing the debate between agency and stakeholder theories of the firm. Journal of Business Ethics, 19(4), 319-334.

Shleifer, A., & Vishny, R. W. (1997). A survey of corporate governance. The Journal of Finance, 52(2), 737-783.

Stefanescu, C. A. (2012). Do board committees' features affect corporate governance disclosure? The case of financial institutions. Economics and Management, 17(2), 768-774.

Sullivan, J. D. (2009). The moral compass of companies: Business ethics and corporate governance as anti-corruption tools. IFC Corporate Governance FOCUS publication, No. 7. World Bank Group.

The Institute of Internal Auditors. (2002). Recommendations for improving corporate governance: Presented to the New York Stock Exchange.

United Nations Conference on Trade and Development. (2003). Selected issues in corporate governance: Regional and country experiences. United Nations. https://unctad.org/fr/node/30862

Ungureanu, M. (2012). Models and practices of corporate governance worldwide. CES Working Papers, 4(3a), 625-635.

Valletta, R. M. (2005). Clear as glass: Transparent financial reporting. Healthcare Financial Management, 59(8), 58-66.

Wearing, R. T. (2005). Cases in corporate governance. Sage Publications.

Yammeesri, J. (2003). Corporate governance: Ownership structure and firm performance evidence from Thailand [Doctoral dissertation, University of Wollongong].

Zahra, S. A., & Pearce II, J. A. (1989). Boards of directors and corporate financial performance: A review and integrative model. Journal of Management, 15(2), 291-334.

www.ingramcontent.com/pod-product-compliance
Lightning Source LLC
LaVergne TN
LVHW082342200926
848481LV00012B/3420